Mama's Santos:

An Arizona Life

By Carmen Duarte

Arizona Daily Star

Published by the Arizona Daily Star,
A Lee Enterprises Newspaper,
Tucson, Arizona 2014
ISBN: 978-0-9882562-6-2
© 2014 Arizona Daily Star
Tucson.com

All rights reserved.
No part of this book may be reprinted or reproduced in any form,
including electronic form, without the permission of the Arizona Daily Star.

Cover illustration by Tammie Graves,
based on a photo by A.E. Araiza, Arizona Daily Star

Table of Contents

Preface	5
Mama's family lineage	7
Translations	9
Chapter 1: Field of death	12
Chapter 2: Coming to *El Norte*	17
Chapter 3: Trapped by fire	20
Chapter 4: Faith takes root	23
Chapter 5: Childhood tales	26
Chapter 6: The education of Nala	29
Chapter 7: Little cotton picker	32
Chapter 8: The Lunt family	35
Chapter 9: Woman of the house	47
Chapter 10: Ain't we got fun	50
Chapter 11: Angel of death	53
Chapter 12: Fever takes a family	56
Chapter 13: Talking to the dead	59
Chapter 14: The cotton picker	62
Chapter 15: Signs and wonders	65
Chapter 16: Migrants	70
Chapter 17: The river provides	73
Chapter 18: The new deal	76
Chapter 19: Winds of war	79
Chapter 20: The home front	83
Chapter 21: End of war	85
Chapter 22: Uncle Johnny	88
Chapter 23: Coming to Tucson	98

Chapter 24: Cotton pickers and copper miners	**101**
Chapter 25: Daddy's demons	**105**
Chapter 26: My cousin's hell	**108**
Chapter 27: The family doubles its size	**111**
Chapter 28: Life with the cousins	**115**
Chapter 29: Estela and *La Virgen*	**119**
Chapter 30: The 1960s	**127**
Chapter 31: From picker to maid	**131**
Chapter 32: Raúl and Irene	**134**
Chapter 33: Jaime and Richard	**138**
Chapter 34: Raymond and Carmen	**141**
Chapter 35: Life alone with Mama	**144**
Chapter 36: The meaning of it all	**148**
Epilogue	**154**
Awards for 'Mama's Santos'	**157**
Contributors	**158**

MAMA'S SANTOS

AN ARIZONA LIFE

Preface

"Mama's Santos" was a yearlong labor of love for Arizona Daily Star reporter Carmen Duarte.

It began as a simple idea — to illustrate the personal side of Arizona's cotton industry by approaching it from the viewpoint of Carmen's mother, Leonarda "Nala" Bejarano Duarte, who had labored in the cotton fields for much of her 90 years in Arizona and New Mexico.

When Carmen wrote the initial, short story for the Star's annual special section about the area's largest employers, the Star 200, it became clear to Carmen and to her editors that a larger story remained to be told.

Carmen directed her reporting and editing skills to a subject that is unusual for a journalist — her own family.

The result was "Mama's Santos: An Arizona Life" which ran in 36 installments in The Arizona Daily Star from Feb. 13 through March 19, 2000, and was later compiled into a single, tabloid-size section.

"Mama's Santos" is a story of one woman's courage, fortitude and faith. It is the story of Carmen's *familia* and, as many readers told us, it is the story of many families who came to this harsh corner of the country full of promise and rich in resources.

It is a tale of the obstacles they met along the path to that promise, the natural ones of flood, fire and disease; the societal ones of discrimination, economic inequality and even revolution and war.

It is the story of "Nala" who persevered through it all, and of Carmen, who found in her mother's tale a source of strength and renewal of faith in the future.

"Mama's Santos" is a timeless story that adds depth and understanding to the history of Arizona and the people who laid the foundation of the state. To reach future generations and geographic locations and, importantly, to preserve this story that exemplifies the state's extraordinary lives of its ordinary people, the Arizona Daily Star offers this book.

Mama's family lineage

Where it all began

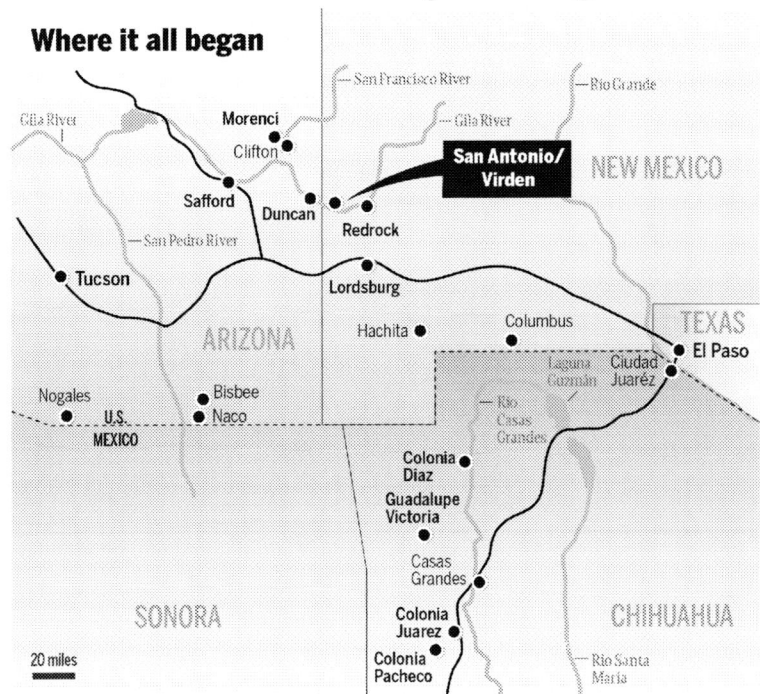

Mama's family

NALA'S GRANDPARENTS:
Florentino and Leonarda Villalba

NALA'S STEPFATHER: **Don Juanito Téllez** ← NALA'S MOTHER: **Dolores** → NALA'S FATHER: **Ambrosio Bejarano**

NALA'S UNCLE: **Andrés** → NALA'S AUNT: **Anastacia Bejarano**

NALA'S SIBLINGS:
- Antonio
- Juan
- Florencia
- Isidro "Chilo"
- Dolores "Lola"
- José

NALA'S BROTHER-IN-LAW: **Manuel Herrera**

NALA'S NEPHEWS & NIECE:
- Raúl
- Irene
- Jaime
- Richard

NALA'S SIBLINGS:
- Gumesinda
- Teodoro
- Angela
- Florentino
- Leonarda "Nala" (Mama)

NALA'S HUSBAND: **Federico Duarte**

NALA'S CHILDREN:
- Raymond
- Carmen (the author)

NALA'S COUSIN: **"Tita"** — TITA'S FIRST HUSBAND: **Ysidoro**

TITA'S SON: **Reyes** — TITA'S DAUGHTER-IN-LAW: **Estela**

TITA'S GRANDCHILDREN:
- Isidoro
- Fernando
- Armando
- Rebecca
- Rey
- Rosie
- Tony

Mama's grandparents were the Villalbas. The two of them, Tata Florentino and Nana Leonarda, are seated in this photo. Florentino holds his granddaughter, Basilia Rodríguez; Leonarda holds her son Pablo. Another son, Andrés, stands between them.

At top is the Villalbas' son-in-law Ignacio Rodríguez and two of their daughters, Dolores (left) and Petra (right). Petra was Ignacio's wife. Dolores later gave birth to Mama.

The other children in the photo, left to right, are Teodoro Bejarano, Juana Villalba and Concepción Rodríguez. Teodoro and Concepción were grandchildren of the Villalbas. Juana was their daughter.

Translations

Abrazo: *embrace*
Abuela, abuelita: grandmother
Abuelo, abuelito: grandfather
Abuelos: grandparents
Adiós: goodbye
Arroz con pollo: rice and chicken
Asaderos: white cheese
Bailes: dances
Bisabuelos: great-grandparents
Boleros: slow, romantic music
Bruja: witch
Cabezón: blockhead
Campesinos: farm workers
Cariño: love
Carnala: sister
Carne asada: grilled beef
Casa: house
Casa de madera: wooden house
Chica: young girl
Chicharrones: cracklings
Chillona: crybaby
Chubasco: severe thunderstorm with wind and rain
Chorizo con huevos: Mexican sausage with eggs
Colonias: colonies
Comadres: female friends; godmother to your child
Comida: food
Compadres: male friends, male and female friends; godfather to your child
Consejos: advice
Consentida: pampered one
Corridos: fast Mexican dance tunes, similar to polkas
Curanderos: healers
Daños: spells
Día de los Muertos: Day of the Dead, Nov. 2, All Souls Day
Don: title of respect
El desgraciado: a disgrace of a human being
El Norte: the North, the United States

El Rancho Grande: the great (large) ranch
Espírtu: the spirit
Familia: family
Fiebre: fever
Frijoles: beans
Gracias a Dios: thanks to God
Gracias a todos: thanks to all
Gran susto: great, sudden shock
Gritos: shouts
Hierbabuena: mint
Hojas de laurel: laurel leaves
Huevos con papas: eggs with potatoes
Ilegales: people who enter the country illegally
La burra: literally, donkey; slang for "dummy"
La vida loca: the crazy life
La Virgen de Gudalupe: the Virgin of Guadalupe
La Virgen: the Virgin
Las Posadas: A Christmas procession in which participants re-enact Mary and Joseph's search for a place to stay
Levántate: arise
Los federales: literally, federals; the Border Patrol
Lumbre: fire
Madrina: godmother
Marihuano: pothead
Metates: concave stones used in grinding
Mi gente: my people
Mi linda madre: my beautiful mother
Mitotes: gossip
Mojados: wetbacks
Molino: a device used to grind by hand
Mueble: furniture
Música ranchera: Mexican folk music
Nana: grandma
Nina: godmother
Nopalitos: cooked prickly pear cactus

Nuestra Señora de la Victoria: Our Lady of Victory
Nuestra Señora del Carmen: Our Lady of Mount Carmel
Papas: potatoes
Papas, tomate and chile verde: potatoes, tomato and green chile
Patrón: employer, landowner
Patrones: landowners
Pollitos: chicks, children
Rancheras: Mexican folk songs
San Isidro: Saint Isidro
Santa Teresita de Jesús: St. Thérèse, (the Little Flower) of Jesus
Santo Niño de Atocha: the Christ Child
Santos: literally, saints; also used to refer generally to images of Catholic saints, Jesus and his mother Mary
Susto: sudden shock
Tata: grandfather
Te de anís: anise tea
Tía: aunt
Tilma: a cloak
Tinas: washtubs
Tió: uncle
Vaquero: cowboy
Vata loca: crazy girl
Vato loco: wild, crazy carefree guy
Verdolagas: purslane (fleshy-leaved, edible plants)
Verdolagas con frijoles: purslane with beans

A summer storm darkens the sky as it sweeps along the Gila River Valley. It was during such a storm in 1916 that a lightning bolt killed Ambrosio Bejarano, my Mama's father. Because of the emotional shock to her pregnant mother, the unborn Leonarda was expected to grow up stupid.

Chapter 1: Field of death

A hard life, a hard land

Mama is preparing to die.

This is nothing new. She started to make these preparations when I was in fourth grade, 34 years ago.

Recently, she had me take her to the Jesus, Mary and Joseph Store on South 12th Avenue, where we picked out the rosary with the shimmering crystal beads she is to be buried with. While there, she also bought a picture of St. Thérèse, the Little Flower of Jesus, in a wooden frame, to add to her collection of *santos*.

She ordered another *santo* — St. Teresa of Avila — that must be shipped from Spain. St. Teresa won't arrive for months. Apparently, Mama is not thinking of dying anytime soon.

In September 1999, Mama celebrated her 83rd birthday with a visit to Desert Diamond Casino, where she lost money, but I came home $500 richer. Mama is in relatively good health and she doesn't complain about being tired, but she has lived a long, hard life.

And she is ready to die. Lately, she has begun praying that God will take her instead of my 13-year-old cousin, Brittany, who has thyroid cancer.

She has her burial gown — a red-and-green replica of the clothing worn in depictions of *La Virgen de Guadalupe*, Mexico's most revered Blessed Mother, the symbol of its war for independence from Spain. My cousin Mary Flora sewed the gown to Mama's specifications.

This dressing up of the dead in the imitation of *santos,* the Christ Child and apparitions of the Blessed Mother is a disappearing tradition among Mexican Roman Catholics. Not many in our family have done it, and Mama will probably be the last.

My grandma Dolores was buried in a white gown and blue robe, modeled on the images you see of Mary, the mother of Jesus, as the Immaculate Conception.

My uncle José Téllez of Safford was buried in his pajamas.

Uncle Joe was a mail carrier and a plumber. He would spend a full day delivering the mail and then head off to fix somebody's leaky pipes in the evening. When he finally arrived home, he would bathe, put on his pajamas and luxuriate in the home and good life that his hard work had built for him and his family.

He now wears his pajamas in eternity — in a better place. We don't just believe that in our family. We know it. So when my mother contemplates death, she does so almost wistfully. She will go to a place where existence is not so hard, where you don't have to struggle to feed your family.

It is a place where there are no family squabbles and there is no tragedy. It is a place where she will finally meet her beloved *santos* and her God.

But before she goes, I want you to know about my Mama, who frankly doesn't understand why anyone would be interested in reading about her.

She finds nothing unusual or heroic about a life spent picking cotton and cleaning miners' dormitories and hotel rooms so her children, nieces, nephews and anyone else who needed her help would have a better life than hers.

I do find that heroic. I hope you will, too.

• • •

I'll begin at the beginning, in 1916, in a field along the Gila River, where Arizona meets New Mexico. This particular field shaped Mama's life before she was born.

It is appropriately a field that has witnessed the blending of three cultures — the ancient one, the Spanish/Mexican one and the North American.

Mama is a U.S. citizen, born here. But her people are from Mexico. She is a mix of the Spanish and indigenous cultures of this region. She prefers to speak Spanish. Her paternal grandfather, we believe, was Apache.

This field, now planted with pecan trees, was originally farmed by the Mogollon who, like the neighboring Hohokam, disappeared more than 1,000 years ago.

This field belonged to Mexico until 1848, but in reality it belonged to no one. When my family first came here in the 1870s, the area was shared, tenuously, with the Apaches.

This river, which flowed muddy, turbulent and undammed in the middle of the monsoon in the summer of 1916, was the border between Mexico and the United States until 1854.

But lines on a map mean less here than cultural traditions and family stories.

Lines between past and present are also unimportant.

My Mama's story is the story of her parents and their parents. It is my story and the story of my nieces who live with me and Mama and my brother.

It is the story of my four cousins Mama raised and the numerous nieces and nephews she loved and guided when they called upon her.

It is about *la familia* and the importance of family. And, most of all, it is about Mama's love — that wonderful emotional glue that keeps us together, no matter what.

She taught us to be faithful to one another and to have faith in God.

So I will draw no lines between the natural world and the religious, or supernatural, one. These lines, too, don't exist for my family.

My Mama talks to her *santos*. She prays for miracles and has witnessed some. My Uncle Johnny saw *La Virgen de Guadalupe* while surrounded by German troops in a foxhole during World War II.

My cousins, the Ruíz family in Phoenix, talk to *La Virgen* regularly. *La Virgen* has appeared to Estela Ruíz. She and her husband, Reyes, and their sons have turned their home in South Phoenix into a shrine. The shrine has become a site of international pilgrimage and doing her work has become their life.

So — no lines.

I will let my mother tell this story, as much as possible, and in order to understand it you will have to get rid of some of your preconceptions.

In the literature of Spanish-speaking people, there is a tradition called magical realism. It recognizes that what is real is often quite different from what is true in a literal sense.

This is the real story of my mother and my family. If, at times, it does not ring true to you, you must remember how it begins, in a field along the Gila River, in a place with no physical boundaries, to a family that recognizes no lines between cultures, no lines between past and present, no lines between the natural and the supernatural.

It begins with a bolt of lightning.

• • •

I have brought my Mama to this field to begin telling the story. It is a hot July afternoon in 1999, with the monsoon clouds in the distance and the air crackling with electricity.

Standing by the Gila River, Mama, Leonarda Bejarano Duarte, looks out onto pecan groves that once were fields of maize her father irrigated two months before she was born, 83 years ago. Immense cottonwoods and willow trees stretching more than 100 feet high line the banks of the river, which flows muddy brown from summer rains.

The field is in Virden, N.M., which borders Duncan, Ariz. — a fertile valley where my Mama grew up toiling in the cotton fields for the *patrones.*

Mama's cousin and childhood friend, Cruz "Tita" García, 86, is here with her. Tita lives about two miles from this pecan grove. Tita has never left the small farming community where she and Mama, nicknamed Nala, played, worked, worshiped God and prayed to their *santos.*

Tita lives in an adobe home in Virden she moved into in 1948 — a house she herself renovated, adding three rooms of adobe brick. This is a woman tough as my Mama. She stopped chopping firewood at age 84, at the insistence of her children. Her blood pressure was too high, they said. She shouldn't be picking up the ax to chop logs.

Her granddaughter now chops her firewood. It is that time in her life when children sometimes overrule their parents.

Nala's and Tita's wrinkled faces show wisdom, and their eyes are filled with unending love. The two stand by the Gila River and look onto the grove and beyond where wild grasses, milo, chile, cotton, watermelon and alfalfa grow.

The two women were raised to meet hard work under the sun, in the midst of the four winds. It has been their life. Toiling in fields from sunup to sundown and raising children of their own and children of others has earned them the hearts of many.

They gaze at the pecan trees, standing under a sky spotted with white and deep-purple clouds. More rain is on its way to cleanse and give new birth to the valley. It is under those clouds that my Mama speaks of her father, Ambrosio Bejarano.

• • •

"I never met my father. Everyone said he was a good, honest man who worked hard. He worked the land for the *patrón* and in return he was given half of the harvest.

"He built a two-room adobe house about two miles from this river, near where Tita lives. The front room was very, very large, and that is where the children played, the family slept and the stories were told.

"He owned a number of horses and carriages. He made sure there always was plenty of food in the house. He loved children. My older brothers and sisters would tell me about him. All I have of my father is their memories.

"You see, I was born Sept. 18, 1916, and my father was already dead. He died in July when my Mama (Dolores) was seven months pregnant with me.

"On the day he died, there was a *chubasco*, a sudden, violent storm with harsh wind and rain. He and his oldest son, Dimas, a son from a previous marriage, were working the fields.

"The sky turned black and it started thundering, and lightning was all around. My father told Dimas they had to run for cover. They were running to a nearby cottonwood tree, which had an immense trunk that hollowed out and resembled a cave. But they never made it. As he neared the tree, a big bolt of lightning struck and hit my father. He fell and died in the field.

"The force from the lightning bolt knocked Dimas to the ground. He tried to get close to help my father, but the electrical field from the lightning strike kept him away. He walked full circle before he could get close to the body. The bolt entered at his shoulder and came out his forehead.

"He saw that his father was dead, and picked himself up and ran the same dirt road we traveled to get to this spot.

"Dimas ran home to get the horse-drawn wagon so he could return the body. When he went to get the wagon, my mother saw him and figured *'algo pasa'* (something is happening). Dimas drove off in the wagon, led by a galloping horse. My mother followed running, and then walking, and then running some more.

"Dimas loaded the body onto the wagon and headed home, met by Mama on the road. The *susto*, the emotional, sudden fright, overtook Mama when she saw Papa dead.

"News of Papa's death spread like the winds in the community of about 300 people. The women said the *susto* Mama received naturally would affect the baby in her womb. That's what the women said.

"People believed those wives' tales. So, when I was born, people all assumed I was dumb, slow. They assumed I would grow up stupid. That's what they said."

• • •

So it was. Dolores Villalba Bejarano gave birth two months later to my Mama, Leonarda, a child stigmatized from birth by a wrong and cruel belief — one her own mother held. For much of her life, Mama herself would embrace this belief — that she was *"la burra."*

It is a belief that ends with me, and my brother and my cousins and my brother's children, who have come to know Mama, *tía, abuela,* as a woman of strength and, yes, of wisdom.

**The historical, muddy and occasionally turbulent Gila River sweeps over a diversion dam.
The diverted water is life itself to the fields of Virden, N.M., and points beyond.**

Mama's grandparents envisioned lush fields in the Gila Valley like these worked by Gabriel Blanco and his coworkers. Photo by A.E. Araiza, Arizona Daily Star.

Chapter 2: Coming to *El Norte*

Death tugged at Gila settlers elbows

The lightning bolt that killed my grandfather branded my mother.

At birth, she was named Leonarda Villalba Bejarano, in honor of her grandmother. She also took her grandmother's nickname, Nala.

But she would have to bear another nickname — *la burra* — through much of her life.

Her own mother, Dolores, believed that the *gran susto*, the great shock of hearing about her husband's death, had harmed the child in her womb. She would send her into the fields, or keep her at home to cook and clean, rather than send her off to school.

Mama's grandmother, *Nana* Leonarda, would become her namesake's ally and protector against those old wives tales, and against a sometimes-cruel world.

Nana Leonarda reserved a special place in her heart and soul for Nala, the fifth surviving child of Dolores and Ambrosio Bejarano.

The others were, in order, Gumesinda, Teodoro, Angela and Florentino. Two children had died: Maria at age 16 and Gorgonio at 2.

Nana Leonarda and her husband, *Tata* Florentino, not only looked out for baby Nala, they became the widow Dolores' rock. Her husband's death had left Dolores with five mouths to feed.

Dolores' stepson, Dimas, who had eluded death when lightning struck his father, worked the land and became a father figure to his brothers and sisters. But the family leaned heavily on the *abuelos*.

Leonarda and Florentino Villalba would teach Dolores and her children that life is hard and death is a part of it. They lost ten of their own children in their struggle to carve out a living in the fertile valley of the Gila River, whose beauty and promise had lured them from their native land of Chihuahua.

There, their families had lived around Guadalupe Victoria for generations, eking out a living from small farms. They were poor in material goods but bore a rich tradition.

In nearby Casas Grandes, the pueblo had developed a sophisticated pottery tradition long before Christ's birth. The trading trails of those ancient potters and merchants would become the explorer Coronado's path.

Coronado, in 1540, traveled along the Gila River and on up past the buried wealth of copper at Clifton and Morenci, searching in vain for the Seven Cities of Gold.

In 1882, *Nana* Leonarda and *Tata* Florentino traveled those ancient trails, leaving Guadalupe Victoria by horse-drawn wagon and settling in San Antonio, a community of Mexican immigrants founded in 1876 near the present town of Virden, N.M., eight miles from the Arizona border.

The town later established there was first named Richmond, then renamed Virden, in honor of the banker who arranged mortgages for the Mormon families who ended up owning much of the valley.

But San Antonio was the region's first name, and my family was among its first settlers.

On his first trip north, *Tata* Florentino had come alone, leaving behind Leonarda and their firstborn, Petra. He had been enticed to leave subsistence farming in Chihuahua for promised riches in *El Norte*.

The first underground copper mines had opened in Morenci, and their owners sent recruiters into Chihuahua, looking for young, strong men to work the veins. They promised prosperous lives.

It was a wonderful dream, a dream *Tata* Florentino decided to make his. He set out on horseback on a trail that followed the rivers paths through mountain and desert.

When Florentino rode through the wide valley of the Upper Gila to reach Morenci, he, like many heading to the mines, dreamed of returning there to farm.

In Morenci in 1878, Florentino joined hundreds of his countrymen who lived in tent cities and worked for a succession of small mine owners who were soon to be bought out by the Detroit Copper Co. He broke rock, dug tunnels, lived roughly and saved his wages.

By 1881, Phelps Dodge Copper Co. would come to Morenci and become part owner of Detroit Copper. By 1921, PD gained ownership of the entire mining district. Over time, it would produce the greatest wealth of copper in Arizona.

Mexicans weren't the only immigrant laborers. They were joined by others who made a short stop at Ellis Island before heading West with the same dreams. The Italians seemed to favor Morenci, but the Serbs, Croats, Irish and famed Cornwall miners came as well to the growing copper cities of the Southwest.

The Mexicans were immigrants in a technical sense only. This area had long been part of New Spain and became Mexico after its independence was won in 1821.

The Gila River, which gathers its waters in the wild mountains of New Mexico and Arizona, bisects our state today. But it was the boundary between Mexico and the United States in 1848 when Mexico ceded the land north of it. It remained the international boundary until Congress ratified James Gadsden's purchase of the southern portions of New Mexico and Arizona in 1854.

Tata Florentino left the mines after four years and returned to Guadalupe Victoria for his wife and child. Mama heard the story often in her childhood. *Nana* Leonarda was surprised by his return. She had taken to calling him *el desgraciado*, believing he had abandoned his family.

He had not. She was relieved and happy to see her husband.

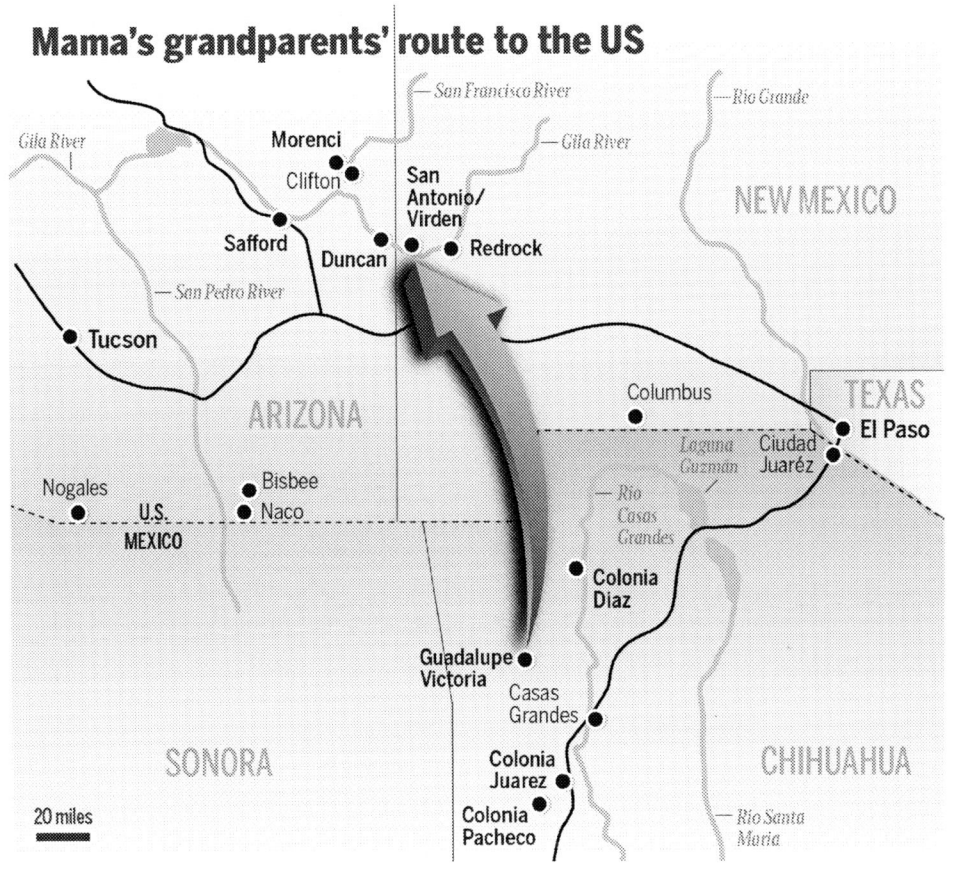

Leonarda Duarte, left, and her cousin Cruz "Tita" García, who died in 2009, visit the San Antonio family cemetery. Photo by A.E. Araiza, Arizona Daily Star.

Chapter 3: Trapped by fire
Building lives, growing families

In 1882, Mama's *Tata* Florentino brought his wife, Leonarda, and daughter, Petra, to settle along the Gila River in New Mexico in the new community of San Antonio. It would be called "Mexican Town" by a later wave of Anglo immigrants.

San Antonio had been founded in 1876 by Cándido Télles.

Télles arrived in the area from Mesilla, N.M., about 1860 to open a freighting business to supply the new mining town of Morenci.

By 1872, he had established the first water rights in the valley, building irrigation ditches to carry water from the Gila to his fields.

Cándido Télles was the grandfather of Don Juanito Téllez, (the spelling of the name changed) who would become Mama's stepfather, the second husband to her mother, Dolores.

In San Antonio, along the Gila River, *Tata* Florentino bought about 10 acres and cleared it of immense cottonwoods — pulling the trunks and stumps with a team of horses.

He built a two-room adobe home. He planted orchards of pears, peaches and plums. He bought cows for milk, cheese and butter. He bought pigs for breeding and slaughter.

Nana Leonarda gave birth to Andrés, Dolores (my grandmother), Juana and Pablo. In all, the couple lost 10 children in *El Norte*.

It was a time when women just gritted their teeth and gave birth with the help of their mothers or the neighborhood midwife.

Complications brought death at birth to babies and the women who bore them. Small children succumbed easily to typhoid, scarlet fever and influenza epidemics. The strongest of the women and babies survived with herbal remedies and lots of prayers to God and the *santos*.

A deep, unquestioning Roman Catholic faith sustained the 24 families in San Antonio, where an adobe chapel was built not long after Cándido founded the community. Its foundation is still visible, next to the family cemetery where Cándido and my other ancestors are buried.

Cándido Télles had not come just to farm. He saw an opportunity to haul wagons and trailers packed with goods to the miners in Clifton and Morenci.

He returned with copper ore, in wagons pulled by his teams of oxen, headed for Silver City, N.M., a major distribution point.

The railroads would soon make his business obsolete, just as cash crops of potatoes and cotton would later make my family's barter-based subsistence farming a relic of the past.

The freighters put in long hours, day after day, hauling goods on winding dirt roads in the valley and up into the mountains, through hot summers, snowy winters and the blessed seasonal rains.

They traveled lands that were home to Apaches, who weren't totally herded onto reservations or shipped off to Florida and Oklahoma until 1886.

Apache blood may have run in the veins of my maternal grandfather, Ambrosio Bejarano, whose father, Gorgonio, is believed to have been a Chiricahua Apache.

So while my ancestral roots are in Chihuahua, my family long ago transplanted itself in *El Norte*, in this land that recently belonged to Mexico. Prosperity was promised to my family and equality was guaranteed, but promises are not always fulfilled and guarantees not always honored.

Two years after my Mama's birth, her widowed mother met and was courted by Juan Téllez, the grandson of San Antonio's founder, Cándido Télles. Juan was fondly called *Don* Juanito. He was a respected, hardworking man whose heart softened when he was around young ones.

His love for Dolores was sincere and large enough to encompass her five children and stepson, Dimas.

When the couple married in 1918, they moved to Duncan, Ariz., about 12 miles downstream from San Antonio.

The family lived close to the Gila River, in a wooden house flanked by farms owned by Sam Foster and the other *patrones*. They hired Mexican laborers to dig potatoes and pick fruit, vegetables and especially cotton, which required immense labor.

The demand for cotton seemed insatiable during World War I. Arizona growers had to compete with mine owners for scarce labor.

Ambrosio Bejarano, my maternal grandfather.

Don Juanito was given the house and a share of the crops for his labor in the fields.

On a winter morning soon after the family had moved to Duncan, my Mama's oldest sister, Gumesinda, 11, began her daily chores at 4 a.m. First, she placed logs into the heater to warm up the house. As all slept, Gumesinda entered the kitchen and began preparing breakfast for the family members who would make their way to the fields by 6.

As Gumesinda prepared *masa* for *tortillas*, sparks from the overloaded heater set a corner of the house on fire.

"Lumbre! Lumbre!" yelled Gumesinda. Dolores and *Don* Juanito jumped out of bed, gathered their children and ran outdoors. As flames quickly engulfed the sunbaked wood of the house, they realized that 2-year-old Nala, as my mother was nicknamed, was not among them. *Don* Juanito grabbed a blanket and ran inside the burning home, crying out Nala's name.

News of the fire traveled quickly to Virden where *Nana* Leonarda and *Tata* Florentino hitched horses to the buggy and rode furiously toward Duncan, a 12-mile trip that normally took about an hour and a half on the rutted dirt road. This time they whipped the horses. *Nana* Leonarda heard Nala was trapped in the fire.

A candle illuminates St. Thèrése of the Little Flower of Jesus. Nala said her santos speak to God on her behalf. Photo by A.E. Araiza, Arizona Daily Star.

Chapter 4: Faith takes root

Nala barely rescued from house in flames

When they heard Nala had been trapped in a fire, *Nana* Leonarda and *Tata* Florentino left Virden by buggy, driving the horse hard.

"My *abuelita* was crying and moaning like an injured cow as they traveled the road to Duncan. The news she received was that I was burned," said Nala, my Mama's nickname.

"They arrived around mid-morning, and I ran barefoot to greet the buggy. *Nana* saw me and began climbing off the buggy before *Tata* brought it to a stop. I ran into the arms of my *Nana*. I loved her and missed her so much."

Don Juanito Téllez, Nala's stepfather, had rushed back into the flames of their burning house with a blanket. He found Nala, frozen in place, standing by a blazing wall. He wrapped her in the blanket and ran out the front door. As he stepped out of the house, the wall toppled. Hearts leaped, and the family knew death was not to take one of them this time.

Nala, her mother, Dolores, and the other children left with the *abuelos* for Virden, where they remained for two days. *Don* Juanito remained, and neighboring men helped him clean out and restore a nearby wooden shack that would become the family's new home. They had to start over, collecting furnishings, dishes and clothes.

Dolores cooked under a tent, and the family slept in the shack until *Don* Juanito built a two-room adobe house, one of four that would eventually be built on the five acres the family acquired through years of laboring in the fields.

All returned to Duncan except Nala, who remained with the *abuelos*. *Nana* Leonarda had insisted on taking care of her, and Dolores gave in, bringing Nala home only on weekends.

Nala grew up carefree and was the light of her *abuelos'* eyes.

She followed her *Nana* and helped with chores, picking up wood for the heater and cooking fires.

Their daily routine included praying the rosary in the evening. *Nana* Leonarda gathered all the area children in her home, including Nala's childhood friend, cousin Tita. All knelt on the packed-dirt floor to pray the rosary beads. Some children didn't like it, but they didn't dare complain.

They learned to pronounce the words and pray in reverence or get pinched. It is a habit that stuck with Mama, a ritual unchanged for 80 years.

Tonight, as she does every night, Mama will kneel at the foot of her bed. Dressed in her favorite blue nightgown, she will whisper her prayers in a soft cadence. A lighted candle will cast her shadow on the wall.

She is a small woman, her black-and-gray hair done up in a beehive. Her shadow looks as if she wears a bishop's miter.

While growing up, we kids would call Mama the archbishop, knowing we had to say it in a low voice or risk getting a shoe tossed at us. The 4-foot-8-inch woman deserved and demanded our respect.

She taught us to fear God as well. On Sundays, she'd wake us long before daylight for 6 a.m. Mass. I close my eyes and hear her voice: "Carmen, l*evántate*." I smell her aroma — always a mix of Avon's Cotillion and the cinnamon scent of Lavoris mouthwash.

Tonight, Mama will sleep in what still seems vast luxury to her — a room of her own with a queen-size bed.

The bed is flanked by night tables filled with dozens of *santos* — saints and images of Jesus and the Virgin Mary in various apparitions.

Tonight, as every night, Mama will pray to God and the *santos* to protect us from all harm and help us during our trials and tribulations.

Tomorrow morning, as every morning, she will sit for two hours in the living room with her rosary, prayer book and prayer cards.

We say she prays for the world. In reality, it is for the extended *familia* —relatives, friends, friends of friends. She'll pray on behalf of anyone who asks and for many who never would.

Every picture, every prayer card, every *santo* tells a story.

The print of *Nuestra Señora del Carmen*, my patron saint, was bought before I was born. It depicts the Virgin with the Christ child sitting on her knee. Below them, souls languish in purgatory. Two angels rescue the soul of one man.

Mama prayed to the Virgin while she was pregnant with me. She promised that if I were born healthy she would name me after her. My name was to be María del Carmen, but the nurses at Tucson Medical Center wrote down "Carmen Mary."

"That's life," said Mama. There is no anger in her voice.

Her hazel eyes twinkle like a child's, but her wrinkled face and hands display the effect of years of backbreaking work in the cotton fields and pecan groves.

Gallons of Corn Husker's lotion saved Mama's hands when they were chapped and bleeding from cuts. The *santos* preserved us all.

**Leonarda "Mama" Duarte, right, and cousin Cruz "Tita" García reminisce about family picnics along the Gila River and childhood pranks.
Photo by A.E. Araiza, Arizona Daily Star.**

Chapter 5: Childhood tales

Mama and Tita reunite after 53 years

Mama's fondest memories are of her six years living with her grandmother, *Nana* Leonarda, and playing with her cousin Tita.

The sweetest moment in researching my family's past came last summer, when I took Mama, who rarely leaves our southside neighborhood, to Virden, N.M., and reunited her with cousin Cruz "Tita" García.

Mama let out a soft gasp when we pulled into Tita's dirt driveway and she saw her cousin for the first time in 53 years.

Mama got out of the car. She and Tita embraced — and immediately the cousins began needling each other about their age.

"Do you need some help walking?" Tita, 86, asked my mother, 83.

"No, I can walk, but you can take my arm if you want," Mama responded.

I knew this was coming. When I had visited Tita a month earlier, she had asked if my Mama still made her own *tortillas*. I confessed that we bought them in plastic bags at the grocery store. "You tell your mother she is not a real woman," Tita said.

The needling gave way quickly to giggling as the two women talked and remembered.

Tortillas, naturally, were one topic. In their childhood evenings after the corn harvest, all would gather outside *Nana* Leonarda's home around large *tinas* and shuck corn for the *tortillas*.

This was not work. It was a time to rest after long days in the fields, catch up on stories and enjoy each other's renditions of *"El Rancho Grande"* and other *música ranchera.*

The children would sip hot chocolate, and the grown-ups drank strong coffee while they cleaned and shucked corn into the quiet, still night.

"My *abuelita* cooked the corn in large pots over the wood-burning stove, and when it was soft we would put it in a *molino*," said Mama, who said some of the women in those days still ground their corn in *metates* with a stone.

"*Abuelita* made corn *tortillas*, and we ate them with *asadero*. It was delicious," said Mama, who was nicknamed Nala.

Tita smacks her lips in appreciation.

"I hated making corn *tortillas* because the *masa* would break up and stick all over my hands," Tita said and laughs with the innocence of a child.

Nala and Tita, who lived with her parents close to *Nana* Leonarda's house in San Antonio, remember sneaking off after morning chores to play and to occasionally misbehave.

The cousins made dishes out of mud, and dolls out of rags. The dolls were lovingly scolded in *Nana* Leonarda's words.

"¡Que chivas son!" (what brats you are) was one of their *abuela*'s favorite lines.

When they were a little older, the cousins took turns grabbing matchsticks, tobacco, rolling papers or *Tata* Florentino's pipe.

They ran to secret hiding places under the cottonwoods to mimic the adults in smoking, before sneaking the stolen items back into place.

"Nala, are you the one who took my pipe," *Tata* Florentino would yell after his pipe miraculously appeared in a place he had already searched.

"No, abuelito. It wasn't me," Nala would say, trying hard not to smile and give herself away.

As years passed, Nala grew closer to her grandmother and started calling her Mama. She loved her weekdays with *Nana*.

On weekends in Duncan, she bore the brunt of brother Florentino's teasing.

"You're not a part of this family. You are an Indian who was abandoned, dumped by the side of the road, and we just took you in," he'd say.

Nala took it to heart. She was the one with the stigma — *la burra* — something her mother did not let her forget. She would cry often and run off to play with make-believe friends.

When Sunday came, Nala was excited to get into the buggy and have her parents take her back to San Antonio and the loving arms of her "Mama" Leonarda.

She loved her own mother. But Dolores did not shower her children with *cariño*. And Nala felt truly at home in San Antonio.

There, she slept with her grandmother, while her grandfather slept in a nearby bed.

There, she was treated like a queen, not having to work hard.

Life was good.

Nala and Tita remember the excitement of summer Sunday picnics: helping *Nana* Leonarda prepare the food; the families gathering in horse-drawn wagons to head for the Gila River, two miles up the dirt road that led from *Tata* and *Nana*'s home.

Tata Florentino's wagon parked with the others along the riverbanks, under the trees.

Brothers tossed ropes over cottonwood limbs for swings and children took turns dropping into the river.

Relatives pulled out their guitars and belted out Spanish tunes while the children played.

Women dried off to begin serving dishes of *verdolagas con frijoles, tortillas, enchiladas, nopalitos con chile, chile con carne* and *arroz con pollo*.

After dinner, the men played poker. Mothers, after cleaning the dishes and packing the leftovers, began to sing.

It seemed to Nala and Tita that they always had to leave the river too early on those evenings, but the workday began at sunrise for these farmers and pickers.

Nala grew stronger in her faith each year. How could she not? All good things — her loving grandmother, the wonderful *fiestas* and picnics — were connected to God and the *santos*.

The children were taught about the special *santos* — *San Isidro*, the patron of farmers; *Santo Niño de Atocha*, the Christ Child, who worked miracles and helped prisoners, mothers and their newborns, miners and the sick and dying.

She would find need for those prayers. Her life was about to get very hard indeed.

Cruz "Tita" García, my mama's cousin.

Nala lived in this home in Duncan after leaving her grandparents in Virden, N.M.

Chapter 6: The education of Nala

*School in Duncan awaits Nala,
but it's a traumatic time*

Nala's world turned upside down at age 8. It was then, on a Saturday, that her mother, Dolores, and family arrived from Duncan. Dolores told Nala to pack. It was time to enroll in school.

Nala's heart was breaking at the thought of leaving *Nana* Leonarda's side, but she didn't cry. While she went to pack her clothes, her *abuela* tried to persuade Dolores to leave Nala with her.

Nana Leonarda promised to enroll Nala in Virden's school. There, Mexican children shared a single classroom, segregated from the Anglo children of what had become a mostly Mormon community.

Some of the Mormon families, strangely enough, were refugees from Mexico.

In the 1880s, when my family left Chihuahua for jobs and land along the Gila River, Mormon polygamists and their families, fearing prosecution, were staging an exodus in the opposite direction.

The Mexican government, under Porfirio Díaz, welcomed the investment, industry and entrepreneurship of the Mormons. Díaz cared little about their family living arrangements, only about his government's cut.

By 1910, when the call for revolution against the dictator Díaz came, Mormons had established several thriving *colonias* around Casas Grandes. They owned lumber and flour mills.

Their prosperity made them a target of the revolutionaries. At about the time of my mother's birth in 1916, the exodus was reversed. The Mormons fled the roving armies of Pancho Villa and the warring generals, back to the United States.

Some families, whom Nala's relatives would work for in years to come, heard of Duncan's fertile farming and ranching valley. They arrived there with the same dreams my family had — buying land and starting anew in the Gila River valley.

Nala's trip was, in contrast, a short one — 12 miles upstream. But it seemed an immense change to the 8-year-old.

While her brothers and sisters played outdoors under the cottonwoods, Nala neatly packed her belongings — three dresses, one pair of brown high-top shoes and underclothes — into a box.

Nala said goodbye to her grandparents and departed for Duncan with her family. The wagon headed to Sam Foster's farm, where her stepfather, *Don* Juanito Téllez, worked as a sharecropper.

Foster, the *patrón*, provided a house for the family and gave *Don* Juanito half of the harvest for his work. That night Nala, a bed-wetter, slept on blankets piled on the floor.

The following morning she dressed for her first day at the Mexican School, a two-story brick building.

Nala put on a white cotton dress with tiny blue and green flowers. She laced up her brown shoes, combed her black hair into braids and sat down to a breakfast of beans and potatoes.

Her mother packed her a bean burro for lunch and off she went, walking a dirt road the distance of about eight city blocks to catch the school bus.

At the bus stop, she joined cousins and friends. It felt good to see familiar faces.

The bus stopped and Nala hopped on. Some 60 children, sitting and standing, crammed the bus by the time it made it to the American School.

The Anglo children walked into their school and the Mexican children walked down the street to theirs.

Nala entered a new world.

The first floor had classrooms for first to fifth grades, and the second floor was for woodshop classes. Nala sat at her own wooden desk — a rarity for her not to have to share.

Mama still remembers the teacher, Mrs. Haney. She was young, pretty and nice. She took roll and pronounced "Le-o-nar-da" correctly. There were 30-some children in the class, and Nala was eager to learn.

In English, Mrs. Haney told the pupils to go to the blackboard. The teacher wrote their names and the children practiced, copying their names over and over with white chalk.

Next came pronouncing words and writing them on the board. Cat. Rat. Nala repeated the words, yearning to learn English.

When lunchtime came, Nala sat on the steps and ate her bean burro. She drank a cup of water from a jug in the hallway.

She then went to the playground, where she saw her first manufactured swing and seesaw set. The children took turns.

Nala practiced writing her ABCs and pronouncing words the rest of the afternoon. When class let out she walked to the American School to catch the bus, feeling good about her first day.

At home, sisters Gumesinda, 17; and Angela, 14, were helping their mother with chores and caring for the youngest members of the family: Antonio, 5; Juan, 3; Florencia, 1; and infant Isidro.

Older brother Teodoro, at 15, routinely spent his days with his *Tía* Petra in San Antonio.

Florentino, 12, took off after school to the river, teasing Nala before he left.

Nala played school outdoors. She wrote R-A-T and C-A-T in the air, pretending she was at the blackboard.

Angela and Gumesinda stared at their sister. "What are you doing?" Angela asked. "I'm playing school," Nala replied, not caring that they laughed.

Nala remembers these carefree moments easily, even 75 years later. They were rare.

**Dolores pulled Nala out of school more often to work; eventually, the fields won out.
Photo by A.E. Araiza, Arizona Daily Star.**

Chapter 7: Little cotton picker

*In school, in the cotton fields,
cruel 'la burra' label haunts Nala*

Nala's excitement about school didn't last long.

On her second day in class at the Mexican School in Duncan, Nala (my Mama's nickname) practiced her ABCs and pronounced words in English, but her mind also drifted to the life she'd left behind in San Antonio, N.M.

She became ill on Wednesday — probably from the sadness she felt because she wasn't with her *abuela*. Mrs. Haney noticed Nala's sad eyes. "Leonarda, are you sick?" Mrs. Haney asked.

Nala was excused from class. She walked the mile to her family's house on the Foster farm and her heart skipped a beat when she saw her *abuelos'* buggy parked near the house.

She ran and then slowed as she neared the house, thinking she needed to look very sick. She walked in and got a huge hug from her grandparents.

"Oh, Dolores, you have to let me take her with me. She can't go to school if she is sick," *Nana* Leonarda told her daughter. *Tata* Florentino smiled: "Here comes the cow for her baby calf."

Nana Leonarda and Nala were together once more, but briefly. On Sunday, she returned to Duncan and school the next day.

The school year passed, and Nala learned slowly. It took her months to learn the ABCs and how to write her name. She learned a few spelling words, and her English improved.

When second grade rolled around, Dolores had other plans for her daughter.

She cited the *gran susto* of learning about her husband's death while pregnant with Nala to justify her actions.

"Nala, you're not learning anything," she told her 9-year-old daughter. "Something is wrong with your brain."

There it was again. That damn cruelty that made my Mama feel worthless. No one was there to protect her from her own mother and that ignorant belief of the *gran susto*.

That belief would haunt Mama through a life of hard labor — hoeing, picking cotton and pecans, and cleaning motel rooms.

She faced 70 years of labor. Hard labor. Menial labor. Piecework. Minimum wage. Or less.

In the years to come, she would stoop and haul and clean and sweat so that her *pollitos*, as she lovingly called us, were fed and clothed.

I don't know how she did it. For a time in the 1960s, her work supported my brother, four cousins and me. That's a lot of *pollitos*. If anyone deserves a spot in heaven, it is you, Mama.

Nala believed she was learning, but maybe her mother was right. She was *la burra*. Nala had heard it over and over and over again from the lips of her mother.

Dolores began pulling Nala out of school more often and taking her to work in the cotton fields. Eventually, the fields won out over school.

Nala worked long hours picking and piling the fluffy cotton in the rows, stabbing her tiny fingers on the dried husks.

Dolores added Nala's cotton to the burlap sack slung over her shoulder. Dolores saw that Nala was a good worker, another child who could help with the family's finances.

She began telling Nala that school was only for boys because they were the ones who needed better jobs to support their families once they married. Girls did not need school.

Nala didn't argue. Her mother was telling her this, so it must be right. But why were her sisters allowed more schooling?

She was not the only child in the fields. Many other Mexican families, especially the newer immigrants who owned no land, made the same hard choices for their children.

Nala was good at the work, and before long she was given her own potato sack to fill.

It took months to clear the fields, but they were picked clean when the Mexicans were through. My Mama can't drive by a cotton field today without criticizing the wastefulness of modern agriculture.

Those machines just don't do it right. And, she argues, the machines took away the opportunity for people to make a very good living doing something enjoyable and healthful.

Nala, you see, learned to love picking cotton. It didn't seem so bad. She loved being outdoors in the midst of the four winds.

And finally, she was good at something in her mother's eyes.

The following school year, her brother Florentino let it slip that Nala and other children were not being sent to school, and a truant officer was dispatched.

One day, Nala was brought in directly from the fields. She was embarrassed — tossed into the classroom dirty and in her work clothes. She had missed a whole year, and Mrs. Haney was no longer there.

She sat with her head hung low, longing to disappear. That was the beginning of a cat-and-mouse game between Nala and the truant officer.

A lot of Mexican-American parents kept their children out of school when the picking was at its peak.

The long-term benefits of an education often came second to a family's immediate needs. School was not an option for many of my relatives.

The children could not stand up to their parents and say *"basta con esto* (enough of this)."

They felt guilty seeing the poverty and hunger at home, knowing they could help. Many simply vowed, as my mother did, that their own children would never be forced to make such a choice.

Nala was bounced from the field to the classroom and back. It went on for years, making it harder for Nala to learn.

Her mother's words — *la burra* — seemed true when it came to reading. She did well in math, though. And she could memorize a spelling list.

Nala plugged away when allowed to attend school, but more and more, she just picked cotton.

The cracking and bleeding lessened as her hands hardened.

Fortunately, her heart did not harden as well.

After enduring a daylong trip from Chihuahua in cattle cars, some Mormon exiles, like Chloe Lunt, above with son Virl, were herded into tent cities set up in El Paso by the government.

Chapter 8: The Lunt family

Bosses also knew poverty, hardship and bias

My relatives were among those who lined up before sunrise behind grower Heaton Lunt's wooden house to work in the onion and potato fields.

"They were there for that dollar a day," recalls Wilbur Lunt. Wilbur was born in 1929 on his father's ranch in Virden.

"My father was real liberal at hiring," he said. "He hired a lot more people than he needed to because he understood their needs. He was having a hard time, too, but he knew poverty."

Like most of the farm owners in the Upper Gila, the Lunts are Mormons — members of the Church of Jesus Christ of Latter-day Saints.

Mormons settled in the Gila River Valley in the late 1890s, two decades after my family had founded San Antonio, N.M.

Wilbur's family followed a more circuitous route, arriving in 1917 from Mexico, via El Paso. His father and uncles, Owen, Ed and Broughton, joined others in buying the Parks Ranch.

Two years earlier, 21 Mormon families had purchased more than 800 acres from a group of Iowa businessmen for $50,000. The Iowa entrepreneurs had formed the Gila Ranch Co., and the company's president was Earnest W. Virden. The town, then known as Richmond, became Virden.

To my family, it must have seemed unfair that the Mormons could just walk in, gain access to capital and take over the valley.

But the Lunts' family history, which mirrored that of other Mormon settlers, is filled with some of the same hardships and discrimination as my family's. It is another tale of strong religious faith and survival.

They, too, moved easily between the United States and Mexico. They have lived in both worlds for more than a century.

As early as 1862, Congress passed an anti-bigamy law, directed at the Mormons. It was not initially enforced, and Mormon settlements prospered and multiplied, spreading across the mountain West.

Settlers and the politicians they elected on the Western frontier began to resent the Mormons' economic and political power as it spread from Utah into Idaho, Arizona, Nevada and New Mexico.

In 1882, Congress passed the Edmunds Bill, which strengthened the anti-bigamy law by denying polygamists the right to vote, hold office or serve on a jury. Polygamy became a felony, and polygamists faced fines and prison.

Federal marshals and local sheriffs began enforcing the law.

In a famous Arizona episode, David King Udall, grandfather of the late Rep. Morris K. Udall, was indicted for polygamy and perjury in 1885. Udall was imprisoned on the perjury charge for five months before being pardoned by President Grover Cleveland.

The Arizona Weekly Journal in nearby Prescott praised his conviction and added:

"We hail with pleasure the dawn of the day when honest individual settlement of our productive valleys shall be protected by the law against the intrigues and grasping designs of the polygamist hordes of Mormonism, sent out from Utah to occupy, control and contaminate our beautiful territory."

As such attacks increased and the church itself began reconsidering its blessing of plural marriages, hundreds of polygamous families fled to Mexico.

Wilbur Lunt's grandfather, Henry Lunt of Cedar City, Utah, was one. He had four wives. At age 63 and blind, he began his journey in 1887 with one family to Chihuahua, Mexico.

Henry's wife, Sarah, 29, who helped run the Lunt Hotel and Stage Stop in Cedar City, provided much of the muscle on the journey, even though she was pregnant and had four sons, 8, 6, 4 and 2, to care for on the trek.

Later, Henry sent for a second wife and their five older children to help with the journey and the settlement in Mexico.

Five of the eight Lunt brothers, including Heaton, above, eventually purchased farms in the Gila River Valley near Duncan. Over the decades, Heaton and Chloe prospered.

• • •

Wilbur Lunt tells me the story on a hot, humid August afternoon in the kitchen of the home his father built in Duncan in 1948.

I had stopped by in the morning to get a feel for the life of the *patrones* who employed my family. Wilbur talked for a while about farming, and then he began to tell me his family story.

His wife, Marian, served us lunch as he talked on. Night fell, but Wilbur kept me mesmerized with his well-rehearsed saga.

Wilbur's religion encourages the study of family genealogy and history. He first heard the tale from his father. He has researched details of it, and he tells it regularly.

For this story, his recollections are supplemented by Henry Lunt's biography, researched by York Jones and written by Evelyn K. Jones:

"They traveled by wagon, crossing the Colorado River at Lee's Ferry. The travel took months, and years for some families. It took my grandfather two years to arrive because he stopped to make a living along the way," Wilbur begins.

"The trip was devastating, and it put my grandfather in poverty. He'd stop in towns, and other Mormon families supplied the Lunts with housing and land to farm so they could eat and earn a meager living.

"My father, Heaton, was born March 7, 1888, on the journey in Moccasin Springs, which is in Northern Arizona. The family stayed on a stock ranch for three weeks before resuming their travels, crossing dangerous, steep mountain trails, boiling tainted water so they could drink it, and digging horses out of quicksand.

"The family continued their journey on down to Deming, N.M., and crossed over into Palomas, Chihuahua, and on down to a Mormon colony called Colonia Díaz," said Wilbur.

Mormon missionaries had begun preaching and establishing settlements in Mexico in 1874, and Colonia Díaz was founded in 1884. When the Lunt family arrived in Chihuahua a few days before Christmas 1889, according to Jones, their caravan included 51 people, 12 wagons, 26 horses, two mules, 19 head of cattle and a dozen chickens.

In Chihuahua, they joined 477 other families in six Mormon colonies. In one of those colonies, Colonia Juárez, was a school with five teachers and 400 pupils.

The Lunts celebrated Christmas and New Year's at Colonia Díaz and continued on to Colonia Pacheco, climbing into the forests of the Sierra Madre on dangerous trails.

They arrived on Jan. 29, 1890, and settled among the loggers and cattle ranchers, 7,000 feet above sea level in a land of pine trees, canyons and mesas.

"My mother's father, William Wallace Haws, was the founder of Colonia Pacheco, and (my) grandfather, Henry Lunt, helped establish it with his families building log houses, a school and church. Orchards and gardens were also planted," said Wilbur.

"It was poverty situations because it was hard to make a livelihood. They had a small acreage of land cleared, and they near starved to death the first winter because the crops froze. Years also brought droughts, but my grandmother was a great innovator and she had cornmeal. Henry Lunt shared his last cornmeal with the starving people.

"One man came and offered a cow for cornmeal, but he wouldn't take the cow. He gave him half his cornmeal, not knowing what he was going to do for the next day," said Wilbur.

The family prayed, and by nightfall received loads of flour from church members in Mesa, in the Arizona Territory.

"My grandmother, Sarah Lunt, was the real hero. She was young with a young family who came from a ranch. She knew cattle and sheep. She and her sons planted corn, beans and potatoes. She and the children milked the cows and made butter and cheese to sell. They also sold horses. She was an industrious woman who, along with her boys, survived and did very well."

**Sarah Lunt provided much of the muscle on her family's long, arduous journey
from Cedar City, Utah, to Mexico. She knew cattle and sheep,
and she and her sons planted corn, beans and potatoes.**

• • •

In 1897, Sarah Lunt bought the Spencer Ranch in Corrales, about two miles south of Colonia Pacheco, and she and her sons left their log cabin for a frame house. Henry, who had developed cancer on his right cheek, remained in the log cabin with two wives, Ellen and Annie.

Annie became nursemaid to Henry, washing his sore with warm water, treating it with carbolic acid and castor oil.

Ellen and Henry had no children together, but Sarah left her young son, Owen, with Ellen, who loved him and schooled him.

On the ranch in Corrales, Sarah and the older boys raised cattle and sheep. Sarah spun wool into yarn and knitted the family socks for the winter. They also began a cheese-making business.

Each year the Mormons sent President Porfirio Díaz boxes of fruit and vegetables, including Sarah's cheese, in thanks for letting them live and practice their religion in Mexico.

In 1899, Sarah and her boys were picking potatoes, which the boys took by wagon and sold at the San Pedro mines, when they spotted smoke. Their house was on fire.

Jones writes that Sarah, as strong as any man, ran to the house and began tossing furniture out the window. Son Parley saved enough flour to last them the year. Broughton raced off on a horse to get help from the neighbors. Wilbur's father, Heaton, 11 at the time, braved the flames and rescued a squash pie that the family ate for dinner.

The homeless family quickly built a shed onto the cheese house. Sarah cooked outdoors in a tepee, and the boys slept in the barn.

Faced with disaster, Sarah enlisted her sons in an ambitious building project — a two-story brick house that would have room to put up travelers.

Her sons worked at the lumber mill and brick kiln in return for building supplies.

More than two years later, Sarah and the boys had completed a house with nine rooms, porches, hallways, a veranda, chimneys, fireplaces, closets and pantries.

Sarah had planned room for Ellen, Annie and Henry, but Henry died of cancer in 1902.

He left four wives and 26 children, who would eventually produce 179 grandchildren.

Henry was buried in the cemetery at Colonia Pacheco. A year later, Ellen died and joined him there.

Meanwhile, a railroad line was built to nearby Colonia Dublan, and railroad operators began advertising hunting trips in the Sierra Madre and stays at the "Lunt Hotel."

"Sarah's hotel became known by travelers, and word spread. She took in famous people — senators and mayors from the United States — who came on hunting trips," said Wilbur.

"Older uncles organized hunting parties, and that's one way the family made a living. There was turkey, deer, antelope and bear in the high country. There also was fishing."

The hunting expeditions became famous, attracting businessmen and politicians from across Mexico, and European visitors as well. It was not unusual to have a baron or a duke in the house.

Sarah became the perfect hostess, costumed in a red dress trimmed with black velvet.

She ran the hotel, the boys worked on nearby farms and the family prospered.

She shared food with the children of widows and women whose husbands had returned to their other families back in the States.

Sarah took in five children from three families, including a Mexican boy who witnessed his father's death during an Indian raid. She raised them as her own until they married.

After losing their home to fire, Sarah Lunt and her sons took two years to build a two-story brick home in Corrales, Chihuahua. It became known as the Lunt Hotel.

• • •

In 1910, political unrest surfaced against Díaz, who, during 35 years as president, welcomed foreign investors and established Mexico's credit, built railroads and drilled oil wells.

But most Mexicans grew poorer and more disillusioned with their government as Díaz and top government officials grew richer.

The cry for revolution was sounded Nov. 20, 1910. Francisco I. Madero headed the bloody rebellion. The rebels had no trouble finding support among the poor for a fair share of the wealth and a democratic government.

Rebel bands captured much of northern Chihuahua, which had the only north-south railroad in the nation.

The rebels seized Ciudad Juárez, across the Río Grande from El Paso.

The Mormon colonies were in danger. Anti-American feeling was growing in Mexico, and the rebels were eyeing the *colonias* as a source of weapons, food and horses.

The Lunts, in their mountain retreat, were initially untouched by the turmoil.

In 1910, at age 22, Wilbur's father, Heaton, married Chloe Haws in a log cabin near the Lunt Hotel. The family continued farming but began hearing more and more reports of rebel raids on the *colonias*.

In 1912, church leaders advised the women, children and elderly to leave.

The people were crammed into cattle cars and were not given water during the one-day trip. A bribe of guns and ammunition bought them safe passage.

"People from El Paso came in automobiles to pick up families," said Wilbur.

"For 90 percent of these people, it was their first ride in an automobile. They were taken to a location prepared by the government. It was an old lumberyard. Families occupied lumber cubicles. The government set up tent cities and helped care for the people," said Wilbur.

Some families left immediately to join relatives or friends. The others lived in the tents for years, enduring the stares of passing townspeople, feeling like animals in cages.

They barely survived. Jobs were scarce and El Paso was filling up with refugees — Mormons and Mexicans, fleeing the increasingly bloody war.

Shortly after the women, children and elderly left, church leaders in Salt Lake City ordered the men to leave as well.

The men gathered at Colonia Juárez and headed for Hachita, N.M., on horseback.

"During the trip, they rode horses and were shot at on a couple of occasions," said Wilbur.

"Men hid their weapons, and many did not have saddles. They threw a blanket over their workhorse. The cowboys helped the farmers survive. This was the rainy season, big cloudbursts.

"There were some devilish messes on this exodus because of the weather. After they arrived in Hachita, they boarded the train to go meet their families in El Paso's tent city.

"Men found themselves penniless and unable to find jobs.

"Some of them immediately went back to Mexico because the authorities didn't tell them, 'Don't go back.' "

The Lunts remained in El Paso. Sarah moved the family out of the tent city into apartments and took in boarders.

"There were up to 10 people living in one room. She was trying to earn enough money to survive in a strange, foreign city. There was malnutrition, and my first brother born in El Paso did survive. My second brother died. Circumstances were very bad," Wilbur said.

Wilbur's father tried to find work using his team of horses and rode to Silver City, N.M., but he struck out. The days passed and the hunger worsened.

Then Heaton heard about a group of men planning to go back into Chihuahua to bring out their cattle. He persuaded his brother-in-law Bill Haws to make the trip with them.

"Each man was responsible for finding his way back across the line and boarding the train. Heaton and Bill hid guns in their pants. The train they got on was loaded with federal soldiers — it was a troop train. The guns were biting them.

"When the train stopped, so folks could run to the bathroom — the bushes — 'We ran to readjust that gun,' " Wilbur's father told him, whenever he recounted the story.

The men made it to Colonia Pacheco and rounded up their cattle. Rebels had taken over the Lunt Hotel and made it their headquarters. It would be burned and then dynamited within the year.

It took the men 10 days to round up about 700 head — they did it quietly, hiding in the cane and corn fields from the rebels.

On the eve of their dangerous gamble to drive the cattle past the rebels to the relative safety of a federal garrison at Mata Ortiz, Heaton and his 12 companions knelt around their campfire and prayed. Success would mean survival for their starving families across the border.

The next morning, fog shrouded the mountains, making it difficult to drive cattle but also difficult for the rebels to follow.

By the time the fog lifted, the cowboys were close enough to the *federales* that the rebels backed off.

Heaton and the group continued moving the cattle to Casas Grandes, where the animals were shipped by train to El Paso.

"This helped a lot of the families. It kept them from hunger. That was their nest egg to survive," Wilbur said.

The barn overflows with alfalfa in this Lunt family photo.

• • •

Heaton found occasional work in El Paso. He used his team of horses to build streets. He worked on survey crews.

But the jobs were not steady, and residents of El Paso tired of the refugees' presence.

Heaton and Chloe briefly returned to Mexico, but they fled back to El Paso after a scary encounter with a rebel faction.

Mexico was no longer safe, and things were tense on the U.S. side of the border.

Pancho Villa and his troops seized Ciudad Juárez. Heaton crossed into Juárez one day and witnessed Villa's execution of his opponents.

Wilbur said his father took him into Juárez one day in 1938, showed him the bullet holes and told him the story:

"The men were lined up and executed by the soldiers. Bullet holes sprayed the Catholic church's walls. The bodies were thrown on a wagon and hauled out of town and dumped into an old well.

"There were so many of them that the blood was running through the cracks of the wagon, down onto the running gears. It was just red, red with dripping blood. Several trips were made as the wagon shuttled bodies from the town to the well."

Despite his bloody reputation, many of the poor supported Villa.

But Villa became the principal villain of the revolution in the United States after he executed 16 U.S. citizens at Santa Isabel and then staged a raid on Columbus, N.M., on March 9, 1916.

The United States sent the Army to pursue Villa into Mexico. The "punitive expedition" needed guides. "There were five young men, my father was one of them, who volunteered to be a guide to take the army of men into Mexico," said Wilbur Lunt.

"My dad and (Gen. John J.) Pershing were on the trail of Villa for the most part.

"Gen. George S. Patton was a lieutenant at the time. He became great friends with my dad. He used to like to camp with him and exchange stories.

"Of course, at that time, my father had no idea in the world that Patton would become the most famous general of all times."

Patton gave Heaton's brother, Edgerton, a pearl-handled six-shooter after Edgerton risked his life in a shootout between rebels and U.S. soldiers at the Rubio Ranch in San Miguelito.

It is reported that Patton told Edgerton: "Any son of a bitch that would stand between two lines of fire, like you did, needs a gun."

Pancho Villa was never captured by the U.S. troops. But the mission ended the cross-border raids. The troops were withdrawn. They were needed for World War I.

"My father was real liberal at hiring. He hired a lot more people than he needed to because he understood their needs," said Wilbur Lunt, who grows cotton on the Gila River Valley farm that his father settled in 1917. Photo by A. E. Araiza, Arizona Daily Star.

...

Heaton returned to his family in El Paso on Feb. 5, 1917.

He went to work for a survey crew along the Río Grande and when that job ended, he traveled to Virden, where his brothers, Ed and Broughton, had bought land. Heaton joined in the venture and purchased 20 acres.

The family packed its possessions, shipping some by train. Chloe was pregnant with their third child, so she also traveled by train. It was a one-day trip on the iron horse. Heaton and their son, Virl, 5, made the six-day, 200-mile journey by wagon.

They stayed with Ed and his family. Chloe gave birth to a boy that April. Two weeks later, Heaton moved Chloe and the boys to their first home, a one-room adobe structure with a tent for a roof.

Five of the eight Lunt brothers eventually purchased farms in the Gila River valley near Duncan.

Sarah Lunt, fearless as ever, moved back to Mexico in the summer of 1918, settling at the ranch in Corrales with two of her eight sons.

She died on Dec. 27, 1921, at age 63, and was buried in her adopted country alongside her husband, Henry, and his first wife, Ellen.

In Virden, the Lunt brothers' families multiplied and the area became known as "Luntville."

Heaton sold his original 20 acres in Virden for more land in Duncan — nearly 100 acres. As he had in Chihuahua, he hired Mexicans to work alongside him and his sons.

Over the decades, Heaton and Chloe prospered and purchased several hundred acres. The Lunt families eventually bought about 1,300 acres — just about all the land on the Arizona stretch of the Gila River, to Duncan proper.

The Lunts also run a dairy, which was established by Heaton's brother, George. Since the 1950s, it has been operated by Broughton's sons, grandsons and great-grandsons.

Wilbur Lunt, continues to farm along the Gila into his 80s. He is in the fields most days when the sun comes up, and he works until it goes down.

Unless, of course, someone should happen by and ask him to tell his family's story.

The Lunt family's return to the US

At age 11, Nala became a family workhorse, taking over household chores.

Chapter 9: Woman of the house

With adult duties, Nala has little time for school

In 1926, Nala's oldest sister, Gumesinda, was dating Manuel Lara. Next in line, Angela, was being courted by Geronimo Castrillo, a man 20 years older.
Young Nala (my Mama's nickname) was about to become the woman of the house.
Angela did not listen when her mother tried to persuade her not to become interested in Geronimo. Dolores thought he was too old for her 16-year-old daughter. But love is love.

Gumesinda was the first to marry. It was a fine celebration, and all wore their Sunday best.

Stepbrother Dimas took the bride and groom to church in his black Buick, along with best man Geronimo and maid of honor Angela.

After the services, Nala, 10, had her first ride in a car. She and a slew of children piled into the Buick, squealing with joy as Dimas took them for a spin.

The community of San Antonio, N.M., and friends in Duncan were invited to Gumesinda and Manuel's wedding celebration at *Nana* Leonarda's house.

Nana Leonarda prepared the food and set out the fine china, silverware and linen that she brought from Chihuahua.

Uncles brought their guitars and couples danced to the *música* — waltzes and lively *ranchera* songs.

The celebration repeated itself months later for the marriage of Angela and Geronimo.

The two older sisters moved into their own adobe homes in the growing family compound in Duncan.

They helped their mother with their younger siblings when they could, but they also worked in the fields and had their own houses to clean.

Dolores leaned heavily on daughter Nala, who at age 11 took over the household chores. By then, Dolores had given birth twice more — to Dolores, known as Lola, who was a year old, and to José, an infant. They would be the last of Dolores' 11 children.

Nala continued to be a workhorse, almost never stepping into the classroom.

When there, *la burra* tried her best. Nala truly wanted to learn.

But mostly she learned to cook and clean. She found the energy and strength to fill a grown woman's role. She attributes it, of course, to God and the *santos*.

She learned from her mother and from *Nana* Leonarda to cook the staples of the family diet — *tortillas*, *huevos con papas* and *frijoles*. She baked biscuits and brewed coffee.

Later, she learned to bake cakes and mouthwatering lemon meringue pies and bread. She cooked with plenty of love, and it nourished her relatives, who labored in the fields beginning at sunup.

In summer, they all came home for lunch at the height of the burning sun and napped before heading back to the fields at 2 p.m., returning home after sunset.

When they were gone, and her mother or one of her sisters cared for the young ones, Nala fetched water from the well and heated it over the stove, pouring it into large wash tins for laundering clothes on a scrubbing board.

She became enraged while washing the pile of diapers, a never-ending chore.

She resented doing the mother's work. She said her anger gave her more energy.

She pressed clothes with an iron heated on the stove.

She made the beds and swept the dirt floor, sprinkling water on it to keep the dust down. The compacted floor was like rock.

Her brothers tended to the vegetable garden, gathered eggs and milked the cows.

Holidays were the only break from ceaseless toil.

Nala's favorite was *La Navidad*, Christmas.

Nala would eagerly climb onto the family wagon with the rest of the children to head to *Nana* Leonarda's in San Antonio for the annual celebration of *Las Posadas* and the novena to *Santo Niño de Atocha.*

The children wrapped themselves in blankets against the chill of morning as the horses pulled the wagons down the winding dirt road into New Mexico.

Christmas brought no presents and no tree. These were frills in a life where you were happy to have food. There were children who drank a glass of water for breakfast when the food didn't stretch during the week.

Nana Leonarda helped widows of the community with the pickled and canned goods that she always had in stock. Nala believed God blessed the dishes at *Nana* Leonarda's celebrations because there always was enough food. The dishes seemed to multiply, as they had in the Bible when Jesus blessed the fishes and loaves of bread.

It took about 90 minutes to arrive at *Nana* Leonarda and *Tata* Florentino's farm in San Antonio. The children ran to the *abuelos*, who eagerly awaited their hugs. Nala and Nana Leonarda felt their special bond during their *abrazo.*

Nala was a little girl again.

She ran off in search of cousin Tita to catch up on gossip.

Tita was going to school in Virden, when she wasn't hoeing and picking cotton, or harvesting potatoes and onions.

The smell of the onions permeated Tita's skin during the picking season. She hated it.

She also hated the way she was being taught at school.

"The teacher wants our parents to teach us how to speak English. But they know our parents do not speak English. They cannot read. How can they teach us?" Tita asked.

Nala quietly listened. She knew the story all too well.

"I'm learning how to write a little, but I'm the only one who can understand it," said Tita, now 14.

Leonarda "Nala" Bejarano stands by the Gila River in Duncan, a town where she and cousin Tita loved going to the movies to see stars such as Fred Astaire and Ginger Rogers, Gene Autry and Shirley Temple.

Chapter 10: Ain't we got fun

*Fiestas' music, solemn rites
brighten two cousins' lives*

Cousins Nala (Mama) and Tita prepared for *Las Posadas* and their annual part in the procession through the dirt roads and paths of 1920s San Antonio, N.M.

The two were poor in earthly goods but rich in their faith.

Nala and Tita loved *Las Posadas* — loved holding the lighted candles and walking in a procession of about 60 people under a blanket of stars.

The children, accompanied mostly by women, proceeded from house to house re-enacting the journey of Mary and Joseph seeking shelter in Bethlehem.

They found no room until arriving at the home representing the inn where Jesus and Mary were finally given shelter.

The marchers gathered in the home and took to their knees. *Nana* Leonarda led a novena, (usually a nine-day series of prayers) that was started and completed that same evening.

It was followed by a second novena to *Santo Niño de Atocha*, who sat on an altar decorated with Christmas ornaments of green, gold, blue and red.

Elderly women had trouble getting up off their knees after the long prayers. Nala's and Tita's knees seemed glued to the floor, but a quick rub and they were ready to go. They could hardly wait to taste the food prepared by their *abuela* and the other women.

All headed back to *Nana* Leonarda's house, where the celebration continued. *Nana* Leonarda's daughters and neighboring women served the flock, easily numbering 300.

Families in the area and from the surrounding hills came to enjoy *Navidad*. Tamales of red chile con carne, enchiladas, soups, rice and chicken dishes lined the tables. Cookies, cakes, hot chocolate and coffee ended the meals where adults and children became one. After the meal, families dispersed and went home.

The religious ceremonies were solemn and far different from the dances and fiestas in San Antonio.

The fiestas brought laughter and music — this was the rural Hispanic version of the "Roaring '20s." Guitars and accordions were pulled out. Uncles, including Pedro Contreras, Crispin Bejarano and Andrés Bejarano, belted out familiar tunes for husbands and wives, boyfriends and girlfriends who gathered at the *casa de madera*, the wooden house built near *Nana*'s especially for dancing.

When Nala and Tita grew older, they joined the others at the fiestas. The cousins would find a corner and sip beer brewed illegally in the nearby hills.

The two became happier with every sip of the liquid made from maize and orange leaves.

The experienced drinkers swallowed whiskey made by bootleggers who lived near *El Cerro de Don Cándido*, named for San Antonio's founder, Cándido Télles. It is now called Kanister Peak, for a man who homesteaded nearby.

Tita remembers a dance when a bad batch of beer made the men deathly ill.

Nana Leonarda treated half the community with her home remedies.

The dances were also a time to make money. Nala said relatives sold enchiladas for 25 cents a plate during the dances. *Los bailes* were held twice a month.

When they visited in July, Tita and Nala roared with laughter recalling how they and the other children would have their own dances. They made music by banging cans. Someone would sing, and boys would ask the girls to waltz.

They were in heaven when Nala's mother, Dolores, bought a phonograph for her older daughters and they played records. "Now we were dancing in style. We had a real orchestra," said Nala, laughing so hard that she had trouble catching her breath.

Childhood was brief. Nala, at 12, and Tita, at 15, worked like adults. Some girls their age were already married.

But Nala slipped back into a childlike freedom with *Nana* Leonarda. It was with her *abuela* that she tasted her first hamburger at the Greenlee County Fair, an event both went to each year. *Nana* Leonarda loved the burgers and would share one with her granddaughter. She could not afford two.

Nala and Tita also loved going to the Duncan Theatre when they could spare 10 cents.

Nala remembers seeing her first silent motion picture with her *abuela*.

Later, she would enjoy the wondrous talking pictures. Her favorites were Gene Autry, John Wayne, Clark Gable, Fred Astaire, Ginger Rogers, Roy Rogers and the child star Shirley Temple.

The movie screen invited them to worlds much different from their own harsh reality.

Life became especially harsh in the summer of 1929, when an epidemic of fever swept through the region. It struck households, including my Mama's, like the angel of death.

Nala prays to Santo Nino de Atocha, background, along with other santos and religious symbols. Photo by A.E. Araiza, Arizona Daily Star.

**Nala's mother, Dolores Téllez, used every home remedy she knew
to fight her daughter's fever.**

Chapter 11: Angel of death

Herbal remedies are put to the test

In 1929, Nala was stricken with fever. Word traveled quickly to her *abuelos* in San Antonio.

Grandparents *Nana* Leonarda and *Tata* Florentino, once again, quickly readied the buggy.

Nana Leonarda's horrendous wails — similar to those of a wounded cow — let all know that tragedy had struck as the buggy made its way to the home of *Don* Juanito and Dolores in Duncan.

Nana Leonarda needed to by Nala, her *consentida* — her special grandchild, her namesake. Twelve-year-old Nala drifted in and out of consciousness while her weakened body battled the fever for days.

Dolores' herbal remedies, including hot teas made from wild plants and a poultice to sweat out the fever, were not working.

They had always worked before.

"Dios, por que no ahora? Por que?" (God, why not now? Why?)

Dolores kept making the poultices, using the recipe taught to her by *Nana* Leonarda — kerosene oil, sulfur, lard, red mustard and talcum powder.

Desperate to save her daughter, Dolores turned to modern medicine and pulled out tablets sold to her by the kind-faced Anglo peddler who periodically traveled the valley.

Dolores tried everything. She boiled a tea made from rose petals and from other wildflowers.

The teas would strengthen Nala's dehydrated body.

Dolores sliced potatoes and soaked the slices in vinegar to place on Nala's forehead. It would bring some cool relief.

She gave her daughter the peddler's tablets with tea that she had cooled in jugs on the porch.

Nala went back to sleep. A short time later, *Nana* Leonarda awakened Nala and gave her more pills, not knowing her mother had already done so.

Nala went into a deep sleep, a comalike state that lasted hours. Her skin turned pale yellow and all wondered what was happening. The angel of death was near.

Nana Leonarda and Dolores spoke — telling each other that they had given Nala the tablets. Fear took a strong hold of their hearts, and both turned to *Santo Niño de Atocha*. Surely, the Christ Child would hear their cries and return Nala to them. Surely, he would not forsake them.

Nala awoke to find *Nana* Leonarda kneeling by her bed crying. Nala's fever broke. *"Gracias a Dios"* (Thanks be to God). Relatives filled the house to pray the rosary in thanksgiving.

Nala gained strength in the following days, but one strange thing happened.

When *Nana* Leonarda brushed Nala's long, jet-black hair, gobs of it stayed in the brush. Nala lost all her body hair. The hair on her head grew back, but her legs and arms remained hairless.

I can laugh about it now, but when I was a freshman in high school, Mama would not let me shave my legs. "Just give it time. The hair on your legs will fall off like mine did."

So here I was, this obedient Catholic kid who listened to Mama and wondered when I'd have hairless legs.

Then one day my brother, Raymond, told me: "Your legs are really hairy."

You know it's bad when your brother notices. I immediately hopped in the shower with a razor, soaped up my legs and off the hair went.

I broke the news to Mama when she came home from cleaning motel rooms that evening.

"¿Por qué hiciste eso, Carmen?" (Why did you do this?), she asked angrily.

"I had to, Mama. Even Raymond said my legs were too hairy."

Not all in the valley were as blessed as Nala, who lost only her hair.

• • •

Fever spread like *lumbre* — a fire that ravages and destroys.

Nala's brother Florentino came down with it while tending sheep in the nearby hills.

He was nursed by his wife, Mikala, and his mother.

Florentino's fever broke after about four days, but he suffered from rheumatism in his knees until the day he died.

Sister Gumesinda was not so lucky. The fever struck her husband, Manuel, and on top of that he got the hiccups.

Mama thinks the hiccups killed him. The fever made him tired, and the hiccups would not allow him to sleep.

They wrapped him in covers and put him on the wagon for the trip to San Antonio. *Nana* Leonarda would know what to do.

The women went to work making poultices, and *Nana* Leonarda made *un te de anís*, the best cure for hiccups. Anise is still used to treat hiccups.

They also gave Manuel tablets from the pharmaceutical salesman.

After about 15 days, the fever broke, but Manuel was very, very weak. Damn those hiccups. The tea was not working.

Then he stopped breathing.

Gumesinda would not accept it. She ran through the house looking for a mirror.

"He is asleep," she cried. "He is only asleep."

Gumesinda placed the mirror over his face. She waited for a mist to form on it from his warm breath. "It will come. It will form, you'll see," she repeated to *Nana* Leonarda and Dolores. But the mist never came.

And death was not yet finished with my family.

Manuel and Gumesinda's sons, Manuelito and Alejo, also died of fever that swept through the Gila River Valley.

Chapter 12: Fever takes a family

Manuel, finally at peace, is laid to rest in family plot

A profound sadness settled in San Antonio. When Gumesinda lost Manuel, she lost the love of her life. His death left her with two babies to raise alone — Manuelito and Alejo.

The women prayed for the widow. *Tata* Florentino, the community's coffin maker, prepared his granddaughter's husband for burial.

He measured Manuel, whose body lay in a back room of *Nana* Leonarda's house — the room used for religious ceremonies. With the two-week torment of fever and hiccups gone, he looked at rest.

Tata Florentino bought lumber at Duncan's mercantile store and built a simple pine box.

As *Tata* and his *compadres* helped saw the wood and hammer the nails, *Nana* Leonarda looked through material she had purchased at the general store.

She found a large piece of blue linen to line the coffin. She and her daughters made a glue by boiling water and tossing in flour. They cut small crosses out of white lace to decorate the coffin's lining.

Tata Florentino washed Manuel's tanned, muscular body and dressed him in a pair of blue pants and a blue shirt. He combed his black, wavy hair.

Manuel had been a handsome man and a wonderful musician. He had moved to Duncan from Santa Clara, N.M., with his father and widowed sister.

He met Gumesinda at one of the bimonthly dances. Manuel was a self-taught musician and at times earned more money playing at fiestas than he did working the fields.

He made the guitar and violin sing, Mama said. He also learned piano after his widowed sister, who had two sons, met and married landowner George Elmer, who had three children — and a piano.

When evening fell, the all-night wake began with a rosary led by *Nana* Leonarda. People filed into the house to pay their last respects and comfort Gumesinda, who was in a daze.

The following morning, mourners followed the men carrying the coffin to the family cemetery, a 10-minute walk from *Nana* and *Tata* Florentino's house.

Manuel was laid to rest there on a low ridge not far from the Gila River, nestled among low hills dotted with mesquite trees and greasewood bushes.

But death was not satisfied with just Manuel.

Manuel and Gumesinda's sons, Manuelito and Alejo, died of fever within the next seven months.

La fiebre was cursing the valley and its people. Home remedies worked for some and not others.

Nala accepted it as "God's will." She prayed rosaries for Gumesinda, who entered a depression that weakened her body.

Then the fever struck Gumesinda.

Nala remembers her mother, Dolores, talking out loud, arguing with the spirit of her son-in-law. She thought Manuel had come to claim Gumesinda.

"Compadre, ésta no es tu ya. Ésta no te la puedes llevar." (Friend, this one is not yours. You cannot take this one.)

The teas and poultices and patent medicines had no effect on Gumesinda.

Dolores saw her daughter become weaker.

She told her daughter Angela to walk over to the house of Juanita Elmer (Manuel's sister) to phone Dr. Nabors.

Dolores had come to trust the doctor after he safely delivered her son José, who had come two months early. That was the first time she used a doctor for delivery, for anything.

The nicely dressed doctor pulled up in his black car around two in the afternoon at the Sanders' farm, where *Don* Juanito was now sharecropping.

Nala saw the doctor's expression of surprise when he entered their home.

Gumesinda was dressed and up and walking. She had so much fever, he wondered aloud, "Where does she get her strength?"

Nala figured Dr. Nabors knew nothing about God and the *santos*.

The doctor left pills and instructions about caring for Gumesinda.

The following day, Gumesinda dramatically improved. In three more days she was fine, in body at least.

Manuel did not get his way, Nala thought. Her sister did not join Manuel and their two sons in the graveyard on a ridge high above the Gila River, where so many from my family are buried.

Florencia Téllez, left, Carmen and Anastacia Bejarano and Nala attend the body of Isabel Vega, Gumesinda's year-old daughter.

Josie Flores, left, who died in 2008, Irene Romero and Vivian Doherty try to make out the name on a relative's grave marker. Photo by Aaron J. Latham, Arizona Daily Star.

Chapter 13: Talking to the dead

If headstones could just tell family stories

Fever and childbirth account for at least a third of the graves in the family cemetery, but hard labor also exacted a toll.

My relatives were buried in mine cave-ins and struck down in the fields.

Mining and farming have long topped the list of dangerous occupations. It seems strangely appropriate that the first man buried in one of Virden's cemeteries was killed by a load of hay.

Tirso Villalba was something of a family scandal. He showed up in San Antonio, N.M., in 1910, an illegitimate child looking for his father.

That turned out to be my Mama's grandfather, *Tata* Florentino.

Nala's grandparents took Tirso in. He lived with them for about a year until an accident caused his death.

Tirso was hauling hay bales on a flat wagon when a wheel fell off. He was crushed when the load landed on him.

He became the first of about 300 members of the community, many of them my relatives, buried in the cemetery that sits high on a ridge above Virden, overlooking the fields in the flood plain of the Gila River.

More than 100 graves are those of infants who died at birth or were taken by *la fiebre*.

The cemetery had been long neglected when my cousin Petra Rodríguez Mungia undertook its restoration in the 1980s.

Petra's own life was in need of some order at that time, and the cemetery became her place to be alone with her thoughts.

As she straightened the mounds of rocks and built pathways between the rows of the dead, her own life seemed to gain order and direction.

"The dead can stretch out now. They don't have to be huddled under the hundreds of rocks that were scattered all around," said Petra, who lives in nearby Duncan.

This cemetery and a smaller, older one, begun in 1885 adjacent to the church of San Antonio, are where my ancestors, the pioneers of this valley, lie.

Headstones mark the graves of war veterans. Other graves are marked with simple wooden crosses, painted white. Some crosses have names but no dates. Others remain blank.

When I walked among these graves for the first time last summer, I so wanted the dead to talk, to share their remarkable and maybe not so remarkable stories.

But many of the stories and even some of the names are known only to those buried here.

Some birth dates on the tombstones are wrong. Petra's grandfather Ignacio Rodríguez was born in 1876, not 1776.

He died in 1917 because he was a "lover boy, a womanizer," said Petra, smiling.

There is a very strange family tale about Ignacio. He was supposedly bewitched by a *bruja* and lured to his death.

Petra knows many of the stories of those buried here:

• Isabel Mata Bejarano born in 1928 and died in 1961 from gas fumes in a Lordsburg-area mine. He died while rescuing his boss. And he didn't even like the man.

• Frank Rodríguez died shortly after completing a *manda* — a promise to God — by walking 12 miles from Duncan to Virden supporting a 10-foot wooden cross on his shoulder. The cross now marks his grave.

• Contosa Rodríguez died in the early 1900s after falling off the back of a wagon that was returning from a funeral.

• Francisco Vásquez was born in 1928 and built a shrine to *La Virgen de Guadalupe*. He died on Dec. 10, 1981, two days before her feast day.

When I visited the cemetery and found the graves of Mama's grandparents, I began to cry. Then I came to the grave of my grandfather, Ambrosio Bejarano, who was killed by lightning two months before Mama was born. The tears would not stop.

I felt the tender presence of my family around me.

My timing was right for meeting *Tata* Ambrosio. It was a cloudy, muggy day during the *chubasco* season, almost 83 years to the day my *abuelo* died.

A warmth entered my soul and I felt so at home. I thanked God for paving the moment for me. His hand was in this task.

"Thank you *bisabuelos* for taking care of my Mama, loving her and protecting her as best you could.

"And *Tata*, how I wish you would have lived. I would have loved to have felt your loving arms around me as a little girl.

"I know Mama's life would have been so much different if you had lived. Her childhood would not have been stolen from her so quickly.

"Your grave needs work. I think the family will have to fix you up around *Día de los Muertos.*

And so we did. A work crew of Duartes, Vegas, Bejaranos and Téllezes descended on Virden with rakes, shovels and paintbrushes. We painted and cleaned and laughed. We ate Petra's fine food. We drank a few beers and told family tales.

Funny thing about this family history business: You get to uncover secrets your own mother doesn't know.

Mama wasn't told about her grandfather's illegitimate son until I reunited her with cousin Tita.

"Nadie me dijo," (Nobody told me), she gasped. Then grinned. Both women laughed.

Tita and Mama lived through much — the Great Depression, World War II, illnesses and the deaths of husbands, parents, siblings and, for Tita, the deaths of five children.

Infidelity may measure high on their scale of immorality.

But what the hell, these two old women have seen it all. As Tita told Mama, *"Somos veteranas."* (We're veterans.)

Nala gets a warm hug from nephew José Vega, who died in 2003, at the family cemetery in Virden, N.M. Photo by Aaron J. Latham, Arizona Daily Star.

Nala mounts the old schoolhouse steps for the first time since 1932, but the door is locked. Photo by A.E. Araiza, Arizona Daily Star.

Chapter 14: The cotton picker

Nala, school part as Depression deepens

Nala cooked, cleaned and took care of her younger brothers and sisters day in and day out until she was about 16.

In 1932, as the poverty of the Great Depression deepened in the Gila River Valley Dolores pulled her from school for good.

Nala had completed fourth grade at the Mexican School in Duncan, trying her best to learn. She received no support from her parents and little from her teachers.

"We played most of the time," said Mama.

"I learned my ABCs, math and spelling. I knew a little bit. But most of the day, we played.

"There was a retired teacher who lived next door to the Mexican School. He reported that the children were playing all day.

"Otilio Reyes, (the town barber and a council member) started questioning the practices. New instructors were brought in and the others were let go. I started learning again with the new teachers, but then my mother pulled me out of school."

The Anglo-controlled school system, purposely or not, slighted Mexican students. Their parents, most of whom spoke no English, many of them illiterate, voiced no protest, wrote no letters of complaint.

The separate, unequal treatment for minority children continued for Hispanics until the Mexican School closed.

My cousin Natalia Peraza, the daughter of *Tía* Angela, said that when she was a student at the Mexican School in the 1930s, she was taught math and spelling. "When we went on to the American School, teachers there started complaining because we were behind in reading and writing. Our English was not up to par.

"Complaints began pouring in, and I think it was in the 1940s (actually 1951) when the Mexican School was closed."

After she left the Mexican School in 1932, Mama never set foot there again until last July.

The Duncan Public Library was then housed in the old school building, now just one story and owned by the American Legion. (The Duncan Public Library is now housed in a new building. The American Legion still owns the building that housed the Mexican School and holds its meetings and other functions in the building.)

Mama walked quickly up the front steps and reached for the doorknob, but the building was locked.

She put her head down, turned around slowly and walked away. I felt a tinge of sadness, thinking the doors were closed to her once more.

In her mid-teens, Nala traded cooking and household chores for the cotton sack.

Dolores wanted her daughter in the fields, pulling her weight and earning money for the family.

Nala was good at picking cotton. She walked those rows with her brothers and sisters and hundreds of other Mexican-Americans and Mexican nationals. Day in and day out, the cotton was picked, weighed and dumped into large trailers that hauled it to the gins in Duncan or Safford.

Some people sang *rancheras*, letting out the wonderful *gritos* while they picked. The singing made the days go by faster.

Nala picked 300 pounds of cotton on good days, beating some of the men.

When her sack was full, she lifted it onto her belly and then up over her shoulder to carry it to the weigh station. This caused a hernia that has given her problems all her life.

Her brother Florentino saw how she was hoisting the cotton sack from her stomach to her shoulder and taught her the correct way to lift it without further injury.

"*Carnala*," he'd say, "look at me. You squat and get under the sack. Then you lift it with your shoulder and back muscles."

When the crop was successful and cotton prices were high, pickers could earn up to $7.50 a day, more than some laborers in Morenci's copper mines. But through much of the '30s, workers earned less than a penny a pound.

By the end of 1932, Nala's Mama, Dolores, had separated from *Don* Juanito.

The kind man was left with Juan, Antonio, Florencia and Isidro to raise.

Dolores moved to Safford with the two younger children, Lola and José.

Nala did not like what her mother did and stayed on with her stepfather. *Don* Juanito was a good soul. He had married Dolores and cared for her five Bejarano children.

As if that weren't enough, the well ran dry that same year. The family carried water in buckets from a nearby irrigation ditch.

Nala helped *Don* Juanito, who was working in nearby Franklin, raise the family. She became mother to her younger brothers and sisters.

Little Juan's hunting and fishing skills helped provide for the family.

So did his quick fingers. Years later, Nala learned that he stole chickens from a neighbor to help feed the family.

Nala's sisters, Angela and Gumesinda, helped when they could. They and their families continued to live in the cluster of adobe homes on the acreage *Don* Juanito and Dolores had bought by the Gila River, not far from the fairgrounds.

Their grandmother, *Nana* Leonarda, took turns staying with the families.

Her husband, *Tata* Florentino, had died in 1930 of cancer. Decades of helping support their children's families had exhausted the *abuelos*' financial resources. They had slaughtered all of their livestock for food and had lost the family farm in Virden where Nala had lived and prayed as a child.

But their lives were still better than the migrants who ended up in the valley during the Depression.

Ignacio's body was found in the Gila River with ax wounds; Francisca's son was jailed. Photo by A.E. Araiza, Arizona Daily Star.

Chapter 15: Signs and wonders

Nala has seen and heard some truly bizarre things

There are some things my Mama saw and heard as a child that she is not certain she believes.

My Mama has seen *curanderos* at work. She has heard family legends of *brujas*, witches who lured people to their deaths. She has lived in a haunted house.

Curanderos had special gifts to counter diabolic spells, but they also possessed power to harm.

Some truly believed in their powers, while others scoffed and reminded the faithful to lean on God, their true defender.

My Mama believes and she doesn't believe. Her faith is in God, not hocus-pocus. But she has seen and heard some amazing things. She told me not to write them down.

"They'll think I'm a crazy old woman," she told me.

I assured her you would not.

• • •

At age 5, Nala just watched and listened, wondering what was real. She knew her stepfather, *Don* Juanito Téllez, was sick, but she didn't understand what was causing his illness.

In 1921, in rural San Antonio, N.M., medical doctors were a rare option. Sickness was treated with home remedies, gathered from the fields. Serious illnesses were treated with prayer. Occasionally, my family sent for a *curandero.*

The children were usually shooed outside when the *curandero* arrived. Nala recalls the story, some of which she witnessed, much of which was told to her:

"*Don* Davíd, a *curandero*, was summoned from Lordsburg, N.M., and he arrived at *Nana* Leonarda's house late one evening.

"*Don* Juanito was lying on the bed, and his stomach and legs were very, very bloated. He was so bloated that he could not walk, but yet some force was pulling him from the bed. The grown-ups were holding him down in the bed.

"*Don* Davíd entered the house, and when he walked to the room where *Don* Juanito lay, he let out a yell. '*Qué estan haciendo desgraciados con este hombre?*' (Wretches, what are you doing with this man?)

"The *curandero* sees evil spirits in the form of witches around *Don* Juanito. The spirits have their hands on *Don* Juanito and are pulling him from the bed.

"*Don* Davíd builds a fire, putting a washtub on the embers. The tub is filled with a liquid that *Don* Davíd makes as he said verses that are hard to decipher.

"While this is going on, bloated *Don* Juanito begins to vomit. He vomits a lot of liquid and a substance that is similar to balls of hair. The hair also appears to have bugs. I don't know what it was. The *curandero* mixed veins of chile into the vomit so that the evil would not pass on into another person.

"*Don* Juanito began to calm down, and out of nowhere a hen with lots of baby chicks walked into the bedroom, as if the spirits transformed into their being. The hen and chicks walked in and then quickly walked out and disappeared."

This was Nala's first encounter with *Don* Davíd, an old man with a wrinkled face, a thick white mustache and salt-and-pepper hair, in his role as a *curandero*. He frightened her, but she knew *Nana* Leonarda would not let anyone or anything harm her.

Don Juanito suffered several of these episodes of bloating.

One time, Mama said, *Don* Juanito was lying on the bed, moaning from the pain. His legs and stomach had ballooned once more. Suddenly, *Don* Juanito broke out in a hysterical laugh and looked out the window.

He winked as though he were looking at somebody.

All the women, who stood around his bed, turned their heads. They gasped when they saw what appeared to be balls of fire rolling down a nearby hill. *Don* Juanito recovered once again.

Don Juanito's bloating ceased for good after *Don* Davíd's final cleansing.

Again, it was at *Nana* Leonarda's house in San Antonio.

Don Juanito lay on the bed trying to get up while Dolores and *Madrina* Juana held him down. The *curandero* went to work, as he usually did, starting a fire outside and putting a washtub over the embers.

He mixed his liquids with chile seeds and other things. He mumbled his strange words. *Don* Juanito began vomiting. This time, he threw up a long, long worm. It was about 12 inches long. *Don* Juanito never bloated up again. They say *Don* Davíd put a protection from evil around *Don* Juanito.

The protection, *Don* Davíd said, was against the spells of a woman named Francisca. *Don* Davíd said she was a *bruja*.

The family was quite ready to believe him. They had already gathered evidence that Francisca's spells, whether supernatural or sexual, had caused the murder of Nala's *Tío* Ignacio Rodríguez in 1917.

Nala heard the tales over time from her *Nana* Leonarda.

• • •

Nala's *Tío* Ignacio was quite macho and ruled his home. He worked hard and fathered nine children by the time he died at 41.

Ignacio farmed along the Gila River in Redrock, about 12 miles upstream from San Antonio.

On occasion, Ignacio would abruptly leave the fields, walk home and tell his wife, *Tía* Petra, that he had to leave. It was as though he were being summoned by some force.

Tía Petra — *Nana* Leonarda and *Tata* Florentino's firstborn — would ask, "What are you going to do over there?"

"I just have to go. I'll be back," he'd reply, and off he would ride on horseback.

There was a simple explanation. *Tío* Ignacio was having an affair with Francisca, who lived across the river from the Rodríguezes.

Nana Leonarda believed that this was not the ordinary kind of bewitching. She had always suspected Francisca of being a *bruja.*

Over the years, she related the evidence she had gathered to her granddaughter Nala.

Nana Leonarda said a boy named Manuel, the son of a close friend, saw something strange while hunting in the desert near Redrock one day.

Francisca was carrying a doll made of cloth. She pushed it through the thorns of a mesquite tree and ordered in a loud voice: *"Me traes a Ignacio. Me traes a Ignacio."* (Bring me Ignacio.)

Before nightfall, Ignacio had left for the other side of the river.

The affair lasted quite some time.

Then one day, Francisca's son learned about the affair. He confronted Ignacio and angrily ordered him not to see his mother anymore.

The meetings did not stop.

Then one day, Ignacio rode off abruptly but did not return.

After three days, a worried Tía Petra went in search of her husband, taking her children with her.

Tata Florentino went along.

They found Ignacio's body, floating in the Gila River. Ignacio had large cuts on his head and back. The wounds came from an ax.

Francisca's son was jailed for the murder.

• • •

There had been earlier evidence of spells.

Francisca always carried a box, about the size of a shoebox. She said it contained tobacco.

One day, *Don* Juanito's brother Antonio Téllez and his wife, Rosa, who was Francisca's daughter, entered the home and saw that her mother had left behind her shoebox.

She and Antonio decided to open it.

They had never believed it contained tobacco, and they were right. It contained the evidence of Francisca's dabblings in the occult: dead, dried frogs and tiny cloth dolls punctured with numerous pins.

Antonio was angered and, they say, that anger saved him from his mother-in-law. The rebellious ones, you see, are not harmed by *daños*, spells. Only kind, timid souls must beware.

Antonio and Rosa had never wanted to believe those rumors about Rosa's mother. Now, though, they had evidence.

Both wanted to burn the box and all its contents, but a neighbor warned that such an act would hurt the people represented by the dolls.

Just then, Francisca walked in. "Give me my box," Francisca demanded, glaring at Antonio.

Antonio stood up, holding the box in his hands. He looked at his mother-in-law and said: *"Vieja bruja, no te vamos dar la caja."* (Old witch, we are not going to give you the box.)

Francisca fumed, but Antonio stood his ground.

He and Rosa left with the box.

They took the pins out of all the dolls, hoping to release people from the spells. They lighted a fire and tossed the box and its contents into the flames.

No one knows what happened to the people the dolls represented. Antonio and Rosa just prayed that they did not die.

The last piece of testimony came much later from *Don* Davíd, when he told *Nana* Leonarda that Francisca's spells were the source of *Don* Juanito's illness.

He said Francisca had tried to put spells on Dolores, too. But my grandmother was not one of those timid, kindly people. The spells never worked on her.

• • •

The haunted house was the wooden house on the Sanders farm that the family lived in for three years before building their own home in 1932.

At first Nala was scared to go to sleep in the house, as was the rest of the family. Nala recalls:

"Every night at 9, you could hear footsteps walking up the path to the front door of the house. You heard the front door open, someone walk in and close the door.

"You could hear the footsteps make their way into the kitchen. Cups and plates rattled, as though someone were getting dishes out of the cupboard to eat.

"The top of the stove rattled, as though someone were putting a pot or frying pan on the grill. Then you heard the footsteps walking to the back door, the door opening and closing, and the footsteps walking away from the house.

"All of us heard it. We were all in the house. We'd get scared, but all the grown-ups and the men were around. After about one month, we just got used to it.

"We'd be talking while Mama was sewing, and then we'd hear the footsteps making their way to the front door. None of us felt an evil presence or anything. It was just the noises."

These days, Mama visits a doctor when she is ill. We are 80 years and 350 miles away from these tales of ghosts and *brujas* and *curanderos*.

And so my mother said to me: "Carmen, do you have to write this? People are going to think I'm really crazy. They are going to laugh at me."

"No, Mama, people are not going to laugh at you. There are things that happen in life, and some are explainable and some are not. It's OK. The stories are fascinating. People will like them. You'll see."

"Estas segura?" (Are you sure?) she asks.

"Yes, Mama."

Macho-man Ignacio Rodríguez was the ruler of his home. He worked hard and fathered nine children by the time he died violently at 41.

In this 1918 photo, Mexicans thresh grain in Duncan, but laws later made such help hard to get. Photo courtesy of Wilbur Lunt.

Chapter 16: Migrants

Liberty's beacon rarely shines on the dark-skinned

Families from Mexico poured into the fields of the Gila River Valley from the 1880s on.

For decades, the border was wide open. Farms and mines competed for labor, sending recruiters deep into Mexico.

That began to change during the recession in copper and cotton that followed World War I. Visa requirements and fees were enacted and, in 1925, Congress authorized a Border Patrol.

Resentment of foreigners intensified during the Depression. A repatriation movement gained support. Across the country, half a million Mexicans were deported between 1930 and 1935, according to Thomas Sheridan in "Arizona: A History."

"*Los federales* would break into the houses at night looking for workers from the other side," remembers Nala.

"I had one friend who hid under a bed when the *federales* broke into the house where he was sleeping. There were people on top of the bed and (the *federales*) asked them if there were any *ilegales* there. They said no, and the *federales* left.

"My friend escaped, but he then returned to Mexico on his own because the raids kept happening."

Duncan-area farmer Wilbur Lunt said the Depression-era raids were nothing compared with what came later.

"In the 1950s, when I started farming, they hit you about once a week. They were ornery and they were nasty. And I've had a lot of trouble. And I have some bad words for the Border Patrol. I've been fined by them over nothing. It just aggravates me to no end.

"If we got rid of the Mexican laborers and the foreigners, this country would starve in two weeks.

"Anyplace I go, anything that is being done physically is being done by foreigners, mainly Mexicans," Lunt said.

Lunt was a gracious host on my two visits to his farm. He tells wonderful stories. He and his wife even offered to put me up for the night when we talked on well past dark. But there is a gulf between us.

"We talk about our hired people as if we owned them," Lunt said to me on my first visit.

"It is not derogatory. It's more of an affection — 'That's my Mexican.' The worker was part of the family. They also said, 'I belong to Wilbur. He tells me what to do.' They would say this when other growers approached them for work.

"My father used wetbacks. That term doesn't offend you, does it?"

Well, yes, Wilbur, it does. And you know it. I heard your wife, Marian, tell you the same thing.

In a perfect world, migrant workers would be called people, or by their names.

"Wetbacks." *"Mojados."*

These words remove the human face from the hungry men, women, boys and girls who risk death in a cruel desert, a flowing sewer pipe or the deep Río Grande to come here.

The Statue of Liberty's beacon for the poor, tired, huddled masses is, in reality, quite narrowly focused. It rarely shines on the dark-skinned.

My own newspaper offends me with its choice of words. It doesn't like to use the terms "undocumented people," or "undocumented immigrants," or "people who entered the country illegally."

It uses "illegal entrants," and despite attempts to stop it, "illegal aliens" to save space in headlines. Damn space.

The newspaper means no harm. Wilbur Lunt means no harm.

And Mexicans themselves began using *mojado* when they swam the Río Grande in search of a better life.

But some people use the words to make themselves feel more important than others.

It's almost as if some Americans believe all Latinos were born in one foreign country. And all of the Spanish-named folks working low-paying jobs must be "wetbacks."

No. No. No.

Some, like Mama, are hard-working Americans. They work in the fields, in the mines, in the hotels, in the restaurants, in the textile mills, in the garment industry, in the landscaping business and in construction because that's where they find jobs.

They work to feed their families and send their children to school. They work hard, hoping their children won't have to do what they do.

Yup, the U.S. Border Patrol agents, riding bicycles in my south side neighborhood, are just doing their job — hunting down foreign-looking women, men, boys and girls.

They stop dark-skinned people and ask them for identification. It doesn't matter that those dark-skinned people are war veterans. It doesn't matter that they are Americans whose roots run as deep or deeper in this region than the agents asking them for identification.

At age 11 my niece, Clarissa, a beautiful dark-skinned American with brown eyes and a smile that makes you smile, woke up from a dream yelling over and over: "Hurry, the Border Patrol is coming."

She could not explain why she was repeating those words.

Months before that dream, she asked me, "Tía, Border Patrol can't come onto the school grounds, right?"

I answered: "No, they are not supposed to."

Yet, I could not guarantee that it would never happen.

A Model A Ford powers a buzz saw at the Lunt Ranch, where trees were cleared for farming.

Chapter 17: The river provides

Dust bowl refugees join Hispanics on the Gila

Tightened immigration patrols during the '30s caused growers to look east for the labor needed to pick cotton.

They recruited drought-ruined farmers and pickers from Texas, Arkansas and Oklahoma.

The Dust Bowl migrants headed for the Gila Valley along U.S. 70 — the southern route to California. For some, Arizona was the destination; for others, it was just a stop along the way.

Some ran out of gas and money. Some had plain old bad luck, like the family of grower Wilbur Lunt's first wife.

Mada Ferris, her sister and grandparents came through Duncan about 1933.

"They hit somebody on a horse and the law held them over," said Lunt, sitting in the kitchen of his Duncan farmhouse, grinning at the memory.

"On her grandmother's side of the family was some pretty high-class people; a relative was the territorial sheriff of Oklahoma. They weren't scum by any means. But the Depression put everybody in bad circumstances."

He remembers a verse from those days and breaks into song:

"Dear Okie, if you see Eric, you tell him Texas got a job for him out in Californy. Digging up gold, playing fiddle in the follies," sings Wilbur, his voice trailing off.

Many of the travelers ended up camping in tents or makeshift shacks along the Gila River, alongside Mexican migrants.

"From time to time during the '30s, there were hundreds living around here. I've seen down under the Duncan bridge, maybe 10 camps," Lunt said.

The mighty Gila River continued to sustain the valley.

Nala's younger brother, Juan, was the river's child and an important family provider.

He had been taught by his mother's brother, *Tío* Pablo Villalba — to be a master hunter, fisherman and turtle catcher.

Turtles basking on the riverbank would plop into the water when they heard noise. Juan would walk the river with a stick, listening for plops, poking the muddy bank. When Juan hit a mass, he went underwater and dug it out.

The turtles were gutted and stuffed with potatoes, *hierbabuena*, chile, cilantro, oregano and *hojas de laurel*.

"They were stuffed like chickens. Some turtles weighed up to 10 pounds. My mom would place them in the wood-burning stove oven, and the shell roasted.

"Oh, yeah, oh yeah, it tasted good," recalls Uncle Johnny, his mouth watering as he recalls his Huck Finn boyhood from his south side Tucson home.

Often, while Juan hunted, Nala foraged for wild greens and tender cactus.

Nopalitos, the tiny pads of prickly pair cacti, grew anytime. Wild spinach and *verdolagas* grew in the desert after the rains. The *berro* was a leafy plant — similar to lettuce — that grew along the irrigation canals.

Nala looked for just the right *nopalitos*, the younger, tender ones. She whacked the plant with the knife and tossed the pieces into a pail. She ignored the thorns. They couldn't penetrate her calloused hands.

Nala would burn the thorns over an open fire and scrape them off with a knife.

The *nopalitos* were cut into pieces, boiled and then prepared with eggs, red chile, onions and tomatoes, or ground beef.

When she picked wild spinach and *verdolagas*, Nala washed and then boiled each plant. A frying pan with lard was heated, and the greens were tossed with beans, onions and red chile seeds.

All were served with freshly cooked *tortillas*. Nala loved to eat the nopales raw with a sprinkle of salt, wrapped in a *tortilla*. It had a sour taste, like a pickle.

Nala's uncles, meanwhile, picked up pieces of beef and pork from the Lunt brothers, Ed and Heaton (Wilbur's father), during their slaughters.

Hispanic families prepared tasty dishes from parts the ranchers would otherwise discard.

Nala remembers hearing about fights that broke out over whose turn it was to get the head.

The cheeks were made into *carne machaca* or beef jerky.

The stomach was soaked, and the women would clean it of its fat and prepare it for *menudo*.

The fat was fried into chicharrones.

The tongue was fried and mixed with spices, tomatoes and onion, or chile colorado.

The tails were used in stews.

The family members were thrifty to begin with. The Depression made them all pinch a little more.

They mended homemade clothes, including undergarments.

"Nobody wore shoes, unless you went to church," said Hal Empie, an Arizona artist who ran the drugstore in Duncan during the Depression.

"I sold a lot of turpentine. It was considered a great treatment for people who stubbed their toes or had cuts.

"You mixed turpentine with sugar and put it on a cloth and wrapped the stubbed toe. You used old bed sheets for bandage strips."

People did what they needed to survive. The loaves and fishes (or the turtles and *tortillas*) always seemed to multiply just enough to keep the family fed.

Little wonder that Mama disdains waste. When we were kids, she'd save food we refused to eat and serve it to us again.

"Carmen, no sabes que es tener hambre. Eres tan desperdiciada." (Carmen, you don't know what it is to be hungry. You are so wasteful.)

I tried to clean out the refrigerator when she was not around. Otherwise, we get into shouting matches about week-old leftovers.

Mama's fallback position — feed the food to the birds. Yeah, right, like the birds are going to eat *menudo*.

"Ma, we don't live on the *rancho*," I say.

"God's creatures deserve to eat," Mama said.

Sure enough, the food disappears and birds flock to the empty flowerbed where Mama dumps the *comida*.

She was the neighborhood St. Francis of Assisi — and my back yard became a feeding station for homeless cats.

The yard reeks of their scent. I chase them away. Then Mama dumps more leftovers.

My Mama would win again. *"Ni modo."* (Oh, well.)

In the Depression, government jobs were the salvation of many. Three Civilian Conservation Corps camps like this opened in the Duncan area. Photo courtesy of the Arizona Historical Society.

Chapter 18: The new deal

Walk down lover's lane diminishes life's cares

The Depression in cotton and copper dragged on into the late 1930s.

The young men and women of the Gila River Valley worked hard when they could find work. They were given their rewards on the weekends.

Dances were held just about every weekend, often just small affairs at people's homes.

The big events were held at Lover's Lane, an open-air dance hall on grower Heaton Lunt's property, outside of Duncan proper and not far from Virden, N.M.

Lover's Lane was a road, flanked by cottonwoods, which led down to the Gila River.

Near the trees was a large ramada where dances for Hispanics were held.

Nala was a girl when the Depression began and grew into womanhood during the hard times.

She loved to dance. She and her cousins would dress up in the one or two good outfits they ordered from catalogs or bought at Duncan's stores.

They may not have had a lot of clothes, but what they had was sharp-looking.

At the dance, "The men would pay and the women entered free," Nala remembers.

"We'd sit on benches and were chaperoned by *Madrina* Juana. We had to dance with whoever asked us, even if we didn't want to. *Madrina* Juana made us, because she didn't think it was right to hurt boys' feelings.

"We had certain boys we wanted to dance with and prayed they'd hurry up and ask us before other boys did."

The crowds danced to music played by visiting bands or by Otilio Reyes, the town barber, and his daughter Margaret. Otilio played the violin and saxophone, and Margaret played the piano.

The musicians played a mixture of English and Spanish tunes.

The women and men felt free under the stars. This was not time to worry about the *patrón*, or payday, or the cotton, onion or potato crop.

It was a time for friendships, possibly romance. It was a true getaway from the monotonous harshness of daily life.

It was a time to dance and let their strong, muscular bodies enjoy life. Couples took over the cement slab and artistically moved to *rancheras, corridos, boleros* and also to the jazzy tunes of swing.

It was so good, so wonderfully good.

There were other bright spots during the Depression.

Nala, like so, so many other poor people, regarded President Franklin Delano Roosevelt as a hero.

Before Roosevelt, my family's only contact with the federal government had been the Border Patrol. Now, it seemed, the United States government actually cared about them.

Arizona and New Mexico had the highest proportion of people receiving emergency relief from the federal government, according to Thomas Sheridan in "Arizona: A History."

And the federal government also provided jobs. Three Civilian Conservation Corps (CCC) camps opened in the Duncan area.

Nala remembers one camp in Virden, and two in Duncan — one by the cemetery and the other at the fairgrounds.

Nala's brother Antonio joined the CCC and was among hundreds who worked in the valley building small dams over streams in the surrounding hills.

Her brother Juan joined up and was sent to a CCC camp near Prescott.

Roosevelt, my Mama believes, wasn't just another politician who wanted votes. He believed in the people. He gave them work.

If you want an explanation of how the Democratic Party's New Deal coalition of labor and immigrant minorities lasted so long, ask my Mama.

When I turned 18 in 1974, she told me: "Democrats are for the poor; Republicans are for the rich."

Now I could go vote.

The worst of the economic hard times ended by 1940. The United States, not yet at war, was on a war footing. Copper and cotton roared back.

Now the family had only to deal with the ordinary problems — grasshoppers, aphids and worms infesting the crops, epidemics of disease and periodic floods.

The Gila River had flooded in 1934 and would do it again in 1941, taking out a neighborhood near Duncan's train depot.

It was a Mexican-American settlement known as Chihuahuita.

"There were about 50 families living in Chihuahuita at the time of the flood. They lived in nice wooden homes," said Frank Francese, who was born on his family farm in Duncan the same year Nala was born in Virden.

The growers suffered as well.

"This was one of the best farms in Duncan for a long time. You dig down there 3 or 4 feet and you will find the richest soil in the world. It is buried with this sand and river silt," said Francese.

The river has claimed 20 acres of the Francese farm, and Frank is living in his third house.

In 1941, he estimates, he lost $10,000 worth of crops. "You just borrowed from the bank and called it a bad year. You just went ahead and milked the cows and kept them eggs."

Flood or no flood, life was improving in the 1940s. Any jubilation, however, was tempered by the knowledge that the war in Europe would most likely hit home — every home — very soon.

**Nala at the Coon home, where she was offered a job as a housemaid.
Photo by A.E. Araiza, Arizona Daily Star.**

Chapter 19: Winds of war

Florencia gets tuberculosis, but she's strong

In 1941, Nala's younger sister, Florencia, was diagnosed with tuberculosis.

Florencia was a junior at Duncan High School, on the way to becoming the first of Nala's 10 brothers and sisters to graduate.

But for that to happen, Nala would have to nurse Florencia back to health.

Older sister Angela drove Florencia to Lordsburg, N.M., where she underwent surgery to remove lumps on her neck.

Florencia was then confined to bed for six months. She could not get up, and she needed to be segregated from her family.

Nala and Florencia moved into an adobe house that their brother Teodoro had built near the cluster of homes on the family's acres in Duncan.

Nala bathed and fed her sister. She cooked chicken soup and stews. She kept the house immaculate and boiled every dish Florencia used.

Brother Isidro was in charge of bringing Florencia her daily treat — ice cream that Nala tried to keep from melting with wet burlap sacks.

When not at Florencia's side, Nala kept house for her stepfather, *Don* Juanito, and her brother Isidro. Nala continued to wonder how her mother, Dolores, could have left this good man, who had cared for her 11 children.

The months passed, and Florencia's nagging cough improved. She was getting stronger, and Nala was happy. She had a special bond with Florencia. Nala wished she could have been as smart and as unafraid as her younger sister.

Florencia was a bit of a rebel like their brother Juan. Florencia stood up to those she felt were snobbish. She would slap around boys or girls who would mess with any of her siblings, and she always defended Nala. No one made Nala feel stupid when Florencia was around.

They grew even closer during Florencia's illness.

Once Florencia was healthy again, she went back to school, and Nala was offered a housemaid's job by Martha Coon, a Kansas native and University of Iowa graduate who came to Duncan to teach English.

She and her husband, Stanley, ran the Duncan Mercantile Co. Stanley, a native Nebraskan, was a banker, a grower and a school board member.

All Nala knew was that they were rich. They owned the mercantile store. Their three young daughters would go to universities. Mr. Coon had acquired a lot of farmland.

And they had built a beautiful ranch-style adobe house that was plastered and painted white.

It sat near the county fairgrounds, across the way from where Nala's family lived in the cluster of small adobe houses.

Mrs. Coon offered to pay Nala $5 a week for cleaning, washing and ironing.

"I have never worked in a house before," Nala told Mrs. Coon.

"That's all right. I'll teach you," said Mrs. Coon, who also had taught home economics.

I had to laugh when Mama told me her response. Later, I cried.

Oh, Mama. Yes, you have worked in a house, in many houses. When you weren't toiling in the fields, and later cleaning houses, mining dormitories and hotel rooms, you were attending to the needs of your family and relatives.

I remember when I was going to college, you made sure the house ran smoothly so that I could focus all my time on studying when I wasn't working.

You wanted me to do well. You wanted all of us to do well, no matter what job or career we landed.

You taught us to give our best and be proud of our work. We were your *pollitos*.

Mrs. Coon taught Nala how she wanted the beds made, and Nala did it to her satisfaction. The cleaning and ironing were a cinch. Nala worked four hours a day and then went to pick cotton to earn more money.

In July 1999, Mama and I visited the house where she had worked.

As I drove up to the house, passing 15 acres of rich grazing land, Mama craned her neck toward the *casa*.

"I don't remember these trees," she said, looking at the gigantic black walnut and mulberry trees.

"These trees were not here."

The home's owner, Judy McKinley, kindly allowed Mama to go inside and reminisce.

Mama walked up the steps of the front porch and into the living room. "There's the fireplace," she said, staring at the brick structure that made the living room look homey.

"I used to clean the wooden floors every morning with an oil mop. They had a large piano over here in this corner of the room.

"On this shelf," said Mama, pointing to a wooden shelf set into a wall, "Mrs. Coon had a container with ashes. I began dusting and I was going to throw it out because I thought it was dust and dirt. I went to tell Mrs. Coon and she yells: 'No, no! That's my father,' " said Mama, slowly giggling and then letting out a good, hearty laugh.

It was in this house that Nala learned from Mrs. Coon about the Dec. 7, 1941, Pearl Harbor attack.

"I think we're in a war," said Mrs. Coon when Nala arrived to clean the following day.

Nala's spirit sank. "I felt so sad because I thought about my brothers." They would be going to war.

Nala's brothers Florentino Bejarano, left, and Juan Téllez were caught up in World War II — Florentino was drafted and Juan enlisted. Nala kept praying to God and *Nuestra Señora de la Victoria* to take care of the soldiers.

Chapter 20: The home front

War brings prosperity at home, prayers for loved ones overseas

The war in Europe had begun to heal the economy of Greenlee County before the United States joined the war in 1941.

Copper and cotton roared back from their Depression slumps.

Then, after the attack on Pearl Harbor, the work force was drafted. Uncle Sam came looking for Nala's brothers, just as she had feared.

Florentino was drafted into the Army, and Juan and Isidro enlisted. At age 16, José enlisted in the Navy.

The women in the Gila River Valley worked even harder, some taking over jobs their husbands, brothers and sons left behind.

Nala's sister Angela went to work for the railroad, laying and repairing track in the Duncan area, becoming one of the first female railroad workers.

Women also entered the Morenci mine for the first time and helped keep the ore production moving.

Nala decided to leave her maid's job with the Coon family in Duncan to make more money.

She headed to Morenci, where she moved in with her mother, Dolores.

Dolores, who moved to Safford when she left Nala's stepfather, *Don* Juanito, had moved again. She ran a boardinghouse in the mining town, which was booming once again.

Florencia, whom Nala had nursed back to health from tuberculosis and who had graduated from Duncan High School, moved with Nala.

Florencia got a job as a nurse's aide at the Morenci hospital. Nala beamed when people asked her how Florencia was doing. She was the first in the family to graduate from high school.

Nala and her youngest sister, Dolores, known as Lola, went to work for Phelps Dodge, cleaning dormitories for the miners.

There were several two-story wooden buildings, and each building had about 80 rooms. Nala was responsible for cleaning 18 rooms, and she moved like a dynamo, earning $16 a week.

The mine workers came from all over: Phoenix, Oklahoma, Texas, Mexico. Indians were brought in from reservations. Injured veterans came from across the United States.

After cleaning the dormitories, Nala helped her mother prepare lunch and dinner for the miners, who worked day, swing and night shifts. She made them burritos of chile and *frijoles*, and bologna sandwiches.

Before she and Lola began their day, the sisters always attended 6:30 a.m. Mass and prayed for their brothers and the family.

Nala was happy when she received letters from her brothers. They never mentioned how bad things were at the front, and things were especially bad for Juan, whose front-line division was pushing into Germany.

Nala kept praying to God and *Nuestra Señora de la Victoria* to take care of the soldiers.

She received letters from a boyfriend, Cristóbal Montoya, who also had been drafted into the Army. She had met him when he was in the Civilian Conservation Corps camp in Virden, N.M.

Cristobal wrote Nala a letter from a foxhole overseas on her birthday and enclosed $25. He wrote that he was not able to go shopping, so he wanted her to buy a gift for herself.

Nala went to the town's jewelry store and bought a wristwatch with a gold band.

Florencia wrote Nala's responses to Cristobal's letters. Nala would dictate to her in the evening after Florencia finished her shift at the hospital, where she cared for newborns and other patients with much tenderness.

Florencia, meanwhile, had fallen in love with her boyfriend, Manuel Herrera.

Herrera, from San Antonio, Texas, had been stationed at the CCC camp near the cemetery in Duncan. Florencia met him while watching a movie at the Duncan Theatre.

Florencia had long, black hair, shapely legs and beautiful green eyes. She had her pick of boyfriends. Nala couldn't believe she picked Manuel.

She thought Manuel acted like "a big shot and talked down to people." She didn't know the half of it.

Manuel joined the Navy and married Florencia when he came to Morenci on leave.

As the war progressed and cotton prices continued to soar, Nala left Morenci and moved back to Duncan in 1945, where her stepfather, *Don* Juanito, had continued to work the fields with sons Dimas and Isidro.

Nala moved into an adobe room with a tin roof behind sister Angela's house. She hit the fields, where she earned $50 a week picking cotton during August, September and October.

With workers in short supply, the crop was still being harvested as late as February in some years. Nala was picking up to 300 pounds a day, and a couple of times collected 400 pounds.

Nala came home from hoeing the fields one day to learn that *Nana* Leonarda, Nala's patroness and protector, had died.

Strong and active to the end, *Nana* Leonarda had just walked several miles from her step-grandson Dimas's house, to the home of Nala's *tío*, Andrés.

She arrived, sat down, and died, apparently of a heart attack.

"She is with God now," said Nala. There could be no other place for this woman of great faith.

Her wake was held on the patio of Andrés' house, where her body was laid on a table.

But first, according to her wishes, her children and grandchildren laid her body on the ground.

Nana Leonarda, who with Tata Florentino had helped pioneer farming in the lush valley of the upper Gila, wanted her body to be ceremonially delivered to Mother Earth as her spirit soared to join God and her *santos*.

Dolores and Florencia Téllez wait for a bus with their sister Leonarda in Morenci. Some in the family would remain in the area; others left, settling in cities across the Southwest. Florencia and Leonarda were among those ending up in Tucson.

Chapter 21: End of war

With war's end, families fan out to the bigger cities

As the war progressed, growers found a partial answer to their labor shortage.

"The Duncan area survived because of the German and Italian prisoners of war who were shipped to camps in Lordsburg and trucked in daily to the cotton fields," said Duncan farmer Wilbur Lunt.

Nala's cousin Apolonia Rodríguez García was a teen-ager when she talked to the Italian prisoners of war in the cotton fields.

"There were 10 men to a farm with a guard," said Apolonia. "They would tell us they missed their families. They would take out pictures and show us their kids. Many of them would cry. They didn't want a war. Mussolini made them go to war.

"They would be picking cotton and they would come over and talk to us because they could understand some of our Spanish," she recalls.

Apolonia's family worked for the Lunts, and she and her husband, José, a retired miner, raised their seven children in Luntville, between Duncan and Virden, N.M. The couple still lives there.

During the war, Apolonia wrote about 10 letters to American soldiers each week, something she was encouraged to do by radio disc jockeys and talk-show hosts.

"I'd write my letters after picking cotton all day. My letters were cheerful letters, uplifting letters. We were told at school not to write about deaths or anything sad. I loved to write. I graduated from eighth grade. I was 16 and I was pulled out from school in Morenci.

"The way I see it, it was an experience. I educated myself by reading Modern magazine. I started in 1944.

"I had a friend who told me about a dictionary and how to look up words. I bought my own dictionary in 1948. I learned how to spell, and I love to read. I have about 80 books written by Louis L'Amour."

Like so many other Hispanics who worked in the cotton fields and were not able to finish school, Apolonia simply said: "That was just the way life was."

During the wartime cotton boom, some children attended school and joined their families in the afternoons.

"School was let out at noon, and the buses went to the fields," recalls Wilbur Lunt.

"I loved those Hispanic families," he said, "because Dad could pick 400 pounds, Mom could pick 300 pounds and the children picked their share."

The good economy brought improvement to the valley.

Mama's sister Angela used her extra money to bring electricity to her house and the others on *Don* Juanito's acres.

She also paid for water lines. Now the family could draw water from an outdoor faucet rather than fetching it from the irrigation ditch. She bought linoleum for her home's concrete floor.

Attitudes toward education improved along with the economy. More Hispanic children were attending school.

The principal came to Angela's house several times to try to convince her son Ambrosio that he should go back to Duncan High School after he dropped out in his sophomore year.

"My parents did not say much. You know how it is. We had to work. My mom and dad worked so hard, and I wanted to help," said Ambrosio, sitting in the kitchen of his beautiful home in the foothills of the Santa Catalina Mountains in Tucson.

Ambrosio Castrillo didn't go back, but he made sure his family received schooling.

He continued to work hard. He worked for years underground at the San Manuel mine, earning money to send his wife, Isabel, and his three daughters through the University of Arizona.

The women earned degrees in education and now work for the Tucson Unified School District.

Isabel, Ambrosio's wife, has a bunch of success stories in her family. Her brother, U.S. District Judge Frank Zapata, also grew up in Safford and also picked cotton.

After the war, Nala's sister Florencia and her husband Manuel became parents to Raúl in 1946 and Irene in 1948. Raúl was born in Phoenix, and Irene in San Antonio, Texas. Manuel moved the family from Texas to Phoenix, then to Morenci, back to Texas, and then to Duncan.

They finally settled in Tucson, and Florencia refused to leave. Nala still did not understand what her younger sister saw in Manuel.

The war opened the eyes of young men across America.

Nala's brothers were no different. They headed for the big cities of the Southwest.

Florentino, Juan and Isidro (Chilo) all eventually moved to Tucson. Teodoro had moved to Phoenix during the war, and later went to California. Antonio moved to California.

José stayed in the region. He married Dora Lopez, who died in 2008, and worked in Morenci's mine before settling in Safford. He got a job as a mail carrier. He's the uncle I told you about in Chapter 1, who was buried in his pajamas.

Gumesinda and Lola, the oldest and youngest sisters, stayed in Morenci with their families.

Angela remained in Duncan with her family, but years later left her husband, Geronimo, and moved to Phoenix.

After Florentino landed a job at the Veterans Administration Hospital in Tucson, he drove down to Duncan and told his little sister, Nala, to pack. Opportunity awaited.

Tucson had become a mecca. It was a Sun Belt boom town. An exciting town. But my family would learn that the streets were not exactly paved with gold.

Uncle Johnny's talent for drawing and painting netted him a trip to Nice, France, when he was in the service. Here, he entertains granddaughter Ellen Gilbert. Uncle Johnny died in 2009. Photo by A.E. Araiza, Arizona Daily Star.

Chapter 22: Uncle Johnny

Uncle Johnny grew up tough — and needed it

Mama's little brother, Juan Téllez (Uncle Johnny to me), was a wild boy in more ways than one.

Part Huck Finn and part *vato loco*, Uncle Johnny hunted, fished, fought, stole and charmed his way through life.

He can laugh about anything, except for some of his World War II memories. Uncle Johnny grew up fast during that war. He faced death and he found redemption.

Fortunately, he had grown up tough enough to handle it.

• • •

In his boyhood, Juan was truly the river's child.

"I love the Gila River. In the summertime, I and my younger brother, Chilo (Isidro), and my nephew Ambrosio (Castrillo) would tell our parents that we were going to the river and not to worry.

"They knew we would be all right. We would take off for two or three days. We'd live in the river like savages. We were free and happy. We'd camp out. I didn't have to worry about my mother hollering at me."

Juan's fishing pole was a stick with a cord and hook attached to the end. He'd hook a worm, cast the line and soon catfish and suckers would be frying over a campfire.

The boys ranged along the 12-mile stretch of the Gila from Virden, N.M., to Duncan. They knew every nook and cranny and where the fishing was best.

When they tired of fish, they hunted turkeys.

"The Mormons used to raise turkeys (along the river). They turned them loose in the winter, and by summertime there would be a big flock of turkeys. Sometimes, we'd kill a turkey or two and roast it up. That's how we lived. It was good eating.

"I'd go down and ask Mormon families if I could take vegetables from their gardens. They'd say, 'Yeah, you can get all the tomatoes and cucumbers you want, just don't trample on the plants.'"

On the last day of their adventure, they would go home loaded with fish and turtles. Sometimes they took home a turkey.

Juan had a reputation for knowing how to handle a slingshot – something his *Tío* Pablo had taught him. His pockets were always filled with rocks.

He hunted quail, doves, rabbits and, according to him, even roadrunners.

The game was made into fine soups, mixed with potatoes and vegetables.

Juan's slingshot skills scared him one time.

"I was bringing a cow back home. I wanted the cow to climb out on the right side of a ditch, but she was climbing out on the left side. I got her by the horns and twisted her head, but that didn't work. The cow made me mad.

"I got my slingshot and let a rock rip. It hit her between the horns and she went down. She started shaking. I ran all the way home, about a mile away."

"Dad, you better come and bring a knife," Juan told his father.

"Why?" asked *Don* Juanito.

"I think I killed a cow," said Juan with a gulp. "No," said *Don* Juanito. "You go back. She'll be up."

Juan ran back, wondering if his Papa was right. While he ran, he prayed to *La Virgen de Guadalupe*. The cow was fine, and Juan took her home.

When he wasn't escaping to the river, Juan liked the escape of the serial movies that played at the Duncan Theatre on Saturdays.

Juan had a routine. "During the day I'd catch one of my mother's chickens, and I'd hide it in a canyon that was nearby.

Juan would pick up the chicken on his way to the movies in the evening.

"There was a man named Trader Martin, and I'd sell my mother's chicken to him for 10 cents.

"I'd go to the movies and sit anywhere I wanted to. The Mexicans sat on one side, and the Anglos sat on the other. Those kids knew me, and those kids were afraid of me. Nobody bothered me. There was nothing that I didn't tackle."

After the movie, Juan would walk back to Trader Martin's place in search of Dolores' chicken, and steal it back.

"He had a lot of chickens. Sometimes I wouldn't catch the same chicken I dropped off.

"My mother would see the chicken and say, 'Where did that chicken come from? That chicken doesn't belong here. Juan, do you know where that chicken comes from?'"

"Yo no sé," (I don't know) Juan would reply.

Juan Téllez hunted, fished, fought, stole and charmed his way through life. In his later years, though, he read, watched ballgames on television and prayed the rosary several times a day, ever thankful to *"La Virgen."*

• • •

During the early 1930s, Juan went to work picking cotton, or gathering potatoes and onions.

There were days when he, like many other preteen boys and girls, worked up to seven days in the fields, getting a half-day off on Sunday.

It was their life, plain and simple. The children missed school when their families found it necessary, and Juan became another statistic when he dropped out in the seventh grade.

Juan earned a bigger reputation when word traveled that he'd beat up one of the growers who kept putting off paying him $7 for seven 10-hour days of hoeing and irrigating the cotton fields.

One day, Juan picked up a piece of wood. "You are going to pay me now, or you'll wish the hell you did," Juan told his boss.

Juan began swinging and cracked two of the man's ribs.

In the end, Juan received $10, not $7, for his work and never returned to that farm again.

When kindhearted *Don* Juanito heard what his son had done, he scolded Juan for turning violent.

But it all worked to Juan's advantage. Other growers sought him out as his reputation as a good laborer grew. And they paid him on time.

Eventually, *Don* Juanito could only say: "You sure made a name for yourself, Juan."

Juan stood out. He wasn't afraid to be different. He believed God created all men equal and those who felt they were better were in for a surprise.

He even made stealing work for him.

On one weekend trip to Virden, N.M., to visit his grandparents, he was sent to the store by his *Nana* Leonarda.

While there, he picked up a handful of nails and put them in his pocket.

When he returned, he went to work and built a wheelbarrow. "Where did you get the brand-new nails?" *Tata* Florentino asked Juan.

"I got them from the barn, *Tata*," Juan replied.

The following day *Tata* Florentino did not get the plow ready to head for the fields. He prepared the buggy and told Juan to accompany him to the Virden store.

There, he made Juan apologize to Mr. Orson Merrell for stealing the nails. He left him there to work off his penalty.

Merrell had Juan clean out a chicken coop. He liked Juan's work and asked him to clean a second.

Merrell paid him 50 cents for about four hours' work. "Juan, I want you to come every week and clean the coops, and I'll pay you 50 cents."

When Juan got home, he told his grandfather of his good fortune.

"*Tata*, wasn't that good that I stole them nails?"

"No, it's not good," said Florentino. "You lose a dollar before you steal a dollar. You are not to steal nothing from nobody."

Juan put his head down. He knew stealing was wrong, but he also knew that good luck followed him. He asked God to forgive him that evening during the rosary.

In his teen years, Juan hung around a bar called the Bonnie Heather Inn in Duncan. He was hired to keep the pool hall clean and to rack balls.

He watched and learned, and practiced the game.

In time, Juan earned a reputation for playing pool. In addition to earning $1 a day running the pool hall, Juan earned another 50 cents playing pool and winning.

Unbeknown to Juan, he was being watched by one of Duncan's leaders. James Luther Teague Watters, a native of England who moved to the valley in 1884, saw that Juan had a knack for billiards. Watters served as the town's postmaster, justice of the peace and was a U.S. land commissioner.

One night Mr. Watters told Juan to play a visiting pool hustler.

"We tossed, and I got the break," recalls Juan. "When I got the break, I did pretty good. I made about 45 billiards. You have to make 51. I missed and the man took over and made about 48. It was my turn again, and I won the game. We played about six games, and the man won one. He became angry and took off."

Afterward, Mr. Watters handed the boy $250.

"What's this for?" Juan asked.

"These are your winnings. That's your share. That's what you won. I'm keeping the other half," Watters told him.

Juan felt real, real tall that day.

"I went and bought my dad, I bought him three sets of clothes. I bought him all kinds of clothes from underwear clear to the top. I bought my sister (Florencia) five sets of clothes. I bought my brother (Isidro) five sets of clothes. I bought myself five sets of clothes."

Juan put $175 into the bank. *Don* Juanito allowed Juan to work in the pool hall because he was earning good money.

Ambrosio Castrillo, left, passes the time with uncle Juan Téllez in a Nogales, Son., bar.

• • •

As the Depression deepened, work, even hustling, was hard to find.

Juan and his good friend Eduardo Córdova decided to join the Civilian Conservation Corps, one of the federal job programs created by President Franklin Delano Roosevelt.

They were sent to a camp in Prescott on a bus that stopped at Safford, Willcox, Benson and Tucson to pick up men.

Some 150 men were on board when the bus arrived at the camp, just outside the city of rolling hills and pine trees.

The camps were run military-style, and the men dressed in uniforms similar to fatigues. Juan worked as a truck driver, hauling logs and brush from the forest during cleanups, earning $1 a day.

He said he also made about $5 a week playing pool.

"The camps were about one-fourth of a mile out of town, and us guys would walk into town to the dance halls. All we wanted was to have a girl at our side," Juan said.

In no time, Juan found a steady girlfriend named Nancy to be his date at the dances.

"I used to meet her in town. One time, her grandfather was waiting for me while I was bringing her home. I dropped her off near a church. I never walked her all the way up to her house. I had drunk a couple of beers."

"I want you to pick up Nancy at the house and leave her off at the house. You are not to meet her down the street," Nancy's grandfather said to Juan.

Juan got smart with him.

"Well, young man, I think I'm going to have to learn you a little lesson. You need to be more polite to your elders," said Nancy's grandfather.

Juan said he thought, "This little jerk. I'll knock him on his butt."

"So I hit him, and he didn't budge. Oh, he hit me, and I couldn't see where he was hitting me from."

The elderly man walked home and Juan made it back to camp.

A few days later Nancy persuaded Juan to walk her home and talk to Grandpa.

While waiting in the living room, he heard a familiar noise: "Ta, ta, ta, ta, ta, ta."

Juan followed the noise to the family's back yard and saw the old man hitting a speed bag.

When the old man saw Juan, he stopped his workout.

"So, you finally come to the house, young man. If you ever want to see my granddaughter, you come here and pick her up at home."

"Yes, sir," Juan replied.

Juan stayed in the CCC camp for six months. At age 18, he returned to the Gila Valley and moved to Morenci, where his mother had just moved with his siblings, Lola and José.

Dolores ran a boardinghouse for miners.

Copper was booming again. Juan went to work in the mines, earning $3 a day for 10-hour shifts, seven days a week of backbreaking work.

Young Juan spent his days using a pickax to break rock to lay railroad tracks for the ore cars going to the smelter.

He graduated to powder man, drilling holes to hold the dynamite for blasting.

In that job, Juan earned $4 a day. He gave it his all working, and he gave it his all playing.

He truly lived the life of a *vato loco*, like so many others. After his shift at the mine, he joined the guys at dance and pool halls, some weeks raking in up to $8 playing billiards.

He loved the brawling, drinking and dancing. As America headed for World War II, Juan was young and carefree.

But he would grow up quickly. He married, had a child, enlisted into the Army and was shipped off to fight the forces of Nazism in Europe.

Juan left a wife and a son who was just learning to walk.

He vividly remembers the troop train to the East Coast.

When he got off at one stop in Texas to buy a bottle of whiskey, another man took his seat.

Juan told him to move.

"We're first before Mexicans," said the man in the seat. "Mexicans don't mean nothing here in Texas."

A stranger intervened, telling the man: "Well, you better get up, get off your ass and let this Mexican take his seat."

"Who do you think you are?" asked the Texan.

The stranger pulled back his jacket, and pinned to his shirt was a badge.

The Texan kept his mouth shut, got up and walked away to another seat.

The lawman walked up to Juan and asked: "Are you going overseas to the war?" Juan had been told not to reveal that information.

"No, we are just going to Maryland."

But the lawman knew where they were headed. Juan and the other soldiers settled back in their seats. Juan took a swig of whiskey, passed the bottle to a friend and marveled at the difference a uniform makes.

Juan took in all he could along the way. He saw the Mississippi River overflow its banks. He saw the great city of New York.

And in Europe, he saw and did things he would like to forget.

"I remember Kassel, Germany. It was a railroad center.

"The (Royal) Air Force bombed the area, and everything was destroyed. There were lots of platoons, and the American troops had to go through the bombed town and check for German soldiers. If there were any German soldiers alive, we had to kill them."

In the rubble of a bombed building, Juan found "a baby who had his leg cut off and part of his stomach was out. He was crying.

"I couldn't take him with me. He was suffering and all alone. Sometimes I think about him. I took my pistol and shot him in the head. To this day I remember that baby. He was about 10 months old. God forgive me."

The story does not surprise Lynn McGuire, who served as a sergeant with Uncle Johnny's regiment — the 276th Infantry — and has written a history of it.

McGuire said the bombers had knocked out the air-raid sirens on their first pass over Kassel. Nobody had a chance to take cover.

"Thousands and thousands of civilians were killed. You could smell that city from miles away," he said.

Immediately upon landing in Europe, Uncle Johnny's regiment had been positioned to defend against the last German offensive on the Western front, Operation Nordwind, along the German border in northern France.

It faced the highly trained and experienced German 6th SS Mountain Division. "We were your basic cannon fodder," said McGuire.

The 276th joined the fight on New Year's Eve 1944. "It was hell," said McGuire. "We took 56 percent casualties in 86 days."

Juan camped out in foxholes. It was much different from the campouts he and his brothers and nephews had along the banks of the Gila River where they enjoyed their boyhood.

The war was "the only time I went hungry," he said.

At one point, Juan thought all was lost.

Sitting in a shallow foxhole blasted from frozen ground, Juan was surrounded by German forces and under heavy fire.

"I started praying to *La Virgen de Guadalupe*, and I saw her. She came to me. She spoke: 'Juan Diego, are you afraid to die?'

"No, I am not afraid to die. I just want God to forgive my sins," Juan told *La Virgen.*

The brown-skinned beauty "reached her hand out to me and touched my forehead. She then disappeared.

"A miracle occurred. American troops started coming. There was reinforcement. The troops pushed the Germans back, and the American troops were able to get out of there safely," said Uncle Johnny, his face overtaken by an expression of amazement.

He made a promise to *La Virg*en that when the war was over and he was sent home, he would make a trip to Ciudad Juárez, Chihuahua, and light candles at the church there.

He did, and he gave the priest all the money he had won playing poker and dice on the ship back to the states. The priest and Uncle Johnny knelt together and prayed. "He blessed me, saying: *'Vaya con Dios.'* (Go with God.)

Germany surrendered, Juan toured France, Germany and England as a boxer and an entertainer in a USO show. Juan fought as a middleweight.

• • •

After Germany surrendered, Juan toured France, Germany and England as a boxer and as an entertainer in a USO show.

His talent? He was an artist. He could draw upside-down, and he could talk a blue streak.

"They used to call me Chief, and the captain came to my room one day and said: 'It's time to get up, Chief. I'm sending you to Nice, France.

" 'They are having an entertainment contest, and you are going to win it.' "

He packed and flew off to Nice.

He watched the other acts from backstage.

"There were guys playing guitar. They were good. Guys singing. They were good. And then they had guys tap-dancing. I was the fifth one."

Juan took a swig of cognac before he walked onstage holding a chalkboard.

"God, I must have seen a million people. Christ, it scared the hell out of me. I couldn't even talk."

It felt like minutes before Juan opened his mouth.

"Ladies and gentlemen, I come from a family of five girls and five boys. My mother liked the name Charlie so well, she named all her boys Charlie, except Jack. She named him Juan. That's me," Uncle Johnny recalls of his act.

"All this time I'm drawing upside down and backwards. Oh, everybody was hollering with laughter. I'm drawing rabbits, a squirrel, names and fancy letters," Uncle Johnny said.

After about five minutes, he walked offstage and took another swallow of cognac.

"The people are hollering 'More, more.'"

Juan did an encore, and he won first prize.

• • •

Uncle Johnny has a God-given talent for drawing and painting.

When I was a young girl, he would paint our mailbox silver and write our last name in fancy letters in royal-blue paint.

For years, he did the lettering on signs for President Fruit Stand on South 12th Avenue near West Ajo Way — he'd paint vegetables and the name of the business.

He also painted houses, and when he retired he painted the exterior of my house out of the kindness of his heart.

And for years, when his health permitted, he painted countless times over graffiti scrawled on my backyard wall. Over the years, I've spent hundreds of dollars on paint for my wall.

It would be so great if these kids were as persistent with their schoolwork as they are in flashing their penmanship throughout the 'hood.

I'll never forget reading a 1998 story in the Star when the Sam Hughes Neighborhood, east of the university, was hit by taggers.

A Crime Prevention League work crew almost immediately charged into the neighborhood to paint over the messages.

In my barrio, near Pueblo Magnet High chool, many homeowners have to save their money to buy the paint to cover up messages.

It's either that or wait for the graffiti-abatement program to catch up to your request.

Uncle Johnny never complained about the graffiti. He'd just come over when it appeared and paint over it.

When he was still driving a car, he'd come by every Sunday after Mass to visit Mama, whom he and Uncle Joe would lovingly call *carnala* — a term of endearment for sister.

Uncle Johnny shared his stories for decades each Sunday. I loved to sit and listen as he put on a performance. *Dios, como me reía.* (God, how I laughed.)

As we talk this time, on a hot July afternoon, my 78-year-old uncle is refreshed by a powerful swamp cooler directed at his head.

These days, Uncle Johnny's blood pressure gives him a bit of trouble. In 1971, a stroke paralyzed his left side.

Uncle Johnny exercised for years to regain his strength by squeezing a ball in the palm of his left hand.

When I saw him during his recovery, he would squeeze my hand with his weakened one and make me wince in pain. Then he'd smile and say: "See, I've got my strength back."

Uncle Johnny enjoyed showing off his drawings for my Mama's grandchildren and his own.

A retired civilian employee of Davis-Monthan Air Force Base, he painted missile silos during the Cold War.

He helped out at St. John the Evangelist Catholic Church, where he volunteered as a St. Vincent de Paul Society worker and as a church usher.

He was a sight on Sundays, wearing checkered polyester suits and colorful ties that Bob Hope, I'm sure, could have used in comedy acts.

In his later years, he read and watched ballgames on television.

And he prayed the rosary several times a day, thanking "*La Virgen*" for saving his life.

Florentino Bejarano moved his family into an adobe home near Tucson's rodeo and fairgrounds. Arizona Historical Society photo.

Chapter 23: Coming to Tucson

Nala quickly feels at home in Tucson

When Nala left Duncan, she packed enough clothing to fill one suitcase and said her goodbyes to her sister Angela and her family.

She said goodbye to *Don* Juanito, her loving stepfather. Even with graying hair, he was still the picture of a *vaquero*, sitting tall in the saddle on his horse, Filly.

Sometimes, though, *Don* Juanito didn't sit so tall. He continued to work hard all day, but he had begun drinking heavily at night after Dolores left him.

Luckily, he had a good horse, which carried him safely home when he stumbled out of the bar of Duncan's Bonnie Heather Inn and climbed onto her back.

It was tough for Nala to leave the Gila River. She had played in its waters and grown up toiling in the fields it watered. In this valley, she had cooked and cleaned and prayed and danced under the stars.

Here she had buried her beloved *Nana* Leonarda and *Tata* Florentino.

She would return for a couple of short visits and, more than a decade later, for the funeral of *Don* Juanito, whose body was found lying in the horse corral in 1965.

Nala stepped into her brother Florentino's Chevy and watched the fields of Greenlee County disappear in the rear-view mirror.

A few hours later, she arrived in Tucson, where Florentino, an Army veteran, worked at the Veterans Administration Hospital on South Sixth Avenue.

He hoped to get his sister on the hospital's payroll.

It's the family story — lured by a dream again — this time the promise of a government job with a decent salary, benefits and pension.

Nala believed what her brother told her without question. Tucson was a city of opportunity, a good life away from the fields.

Florentino had just moved his family from a trailer into an adobe house that he'd built on the southern outskirts of town, east of South Sixth Avenue and north of the county fairgrounds, now the rodeo arena.

The home had indoor plumbing — no more showering in tin tubs, no more sitting in an outhouse.

Tucson in the early '50s was a dusty, sprawling little city on the move. The county population would double in this first decade after the war.

The city, through growth and annexation of areas such as the one where my family lived, would more than quadruple its size, from 45,000 to 212,000 residents.

My family lived among Mexican and Mexican-American families who also dreamed of better lives for themselves and their children. Most of the newer immigrants were from Sonora, but quite a few, like my family, hailed from Chihuahua.

And there were a great many *Tucsonenses*, who could trace their families to a time when Arizona was a part of Mexico or even Spain.

There was still plenty of desert and dirt streets.

Families slept outside on cots during the summer. Women washed clothing in *tinas* with boiling water and scrub boards. Many homes had outhouses. Adobes baked in the sun for future building projects.

The aroma of *tortillas* rose from woodburning stoves in the back yards. Everybody spoke Spanish. Chickens cackled, roosters crowed and lively *música ranchera* filled the warm nights.

Nala settled in among her relatives and neighbors — cotton pickers, miners and the blue-collar labor force of the local, state and federal governments.

She felt instantly at home and began praying to God and *Santa Elena de la Cruz*, patron saint of workers, for a job, any job.

Nala stayed with Florentino and his family for months. She helped her brother's wife, Mary, with her four children and two of Florentino's children from previous marriages, whose mothers had died.

Nala filled her days making sure dishes were washed, the house was cleaned and the children were fed and bathed.

She did not understand why Mary's children were treated better than the stepchildren.

She was heartsick when she saw her young nephew, Rudy Bejarano, (who, decades later, would become a Tucson city councilman) eating from a garbage can. There was no need for that, and it ended when she was there.

Florentino picked up applications for his sister from the veterans hospital and the Pima County General Hospital, both on South Sixth Avenue, and filled them out for her.

Nala was admitted into a training program to become a dishwasher at the old county hospital.

She was good at it, of course, and very fast. Her supervisor put her to work cleaning floors and the medical staff's lounge when she was done with her own duties.

Another worker told her: "You are doing too much, and they are taking advantage of you. Don't do it."

"I don't mind, because I like to stay busy," Nala replied.

After a week's tryout, Nala went for a physical examination and waited to be hired. Weeks passed and Nala received no word.

She returned to the cotton fields, where Florentino also labored when he was not working at the hospital.

Young Florentino Bejarano would, years later, drive his sister Leonarda Bejarano — Nala — from Greenlee County to a new life in that city of opportunity, Tucson.

Rudy Bejarano, here with sister Norma, was brought to Tucson and soon was picking cotton.

Chapter 24: Cotton pickers and copper miners

Southside and new work lures more of Nala's clan

Cotton fields blanketed Tucson's southwest side in the 1950s.

The fields spread west of the Santa Cruz River from Ajo Way south past Valencia Road all the way to Mission San Xavier del Bac.

Pecan groves flanked the cotton fields in what is now the community of Midvale Park.

Field hands were still in demand. Hispanic, Native-American and African-American families picked and hoed along the length of the river, from Sahuarita to Marana and north into Pinal County's Red Rock, Casa Grande, Eloy and Coolidge.

Nala's nephew, little Rudy Bejarano, was among the children who accompanied her to the fields. He had been picking with his father before Nala arrived in Tucson.

Nala's brother Florentino had brought Rudy back from Barstow, Calif., where the boy's mother, Hortencia, had taken him to be with her relatives when Florentino went off to war. She died in 1947.

After Florentino was discharged and remarried, he went to get Rudy, who had never seen his dad.

Rudy was brought into a family of strangers. He missed the warmth and love of his mother's relatives and grew up feeling alone.

Rudy said portions of his childhood remain unclear. "Maybe I have consciously closed that part of my life," he said from his westside home overlooking the lush desert property of Pima Community College.

"I do remember some things. I remember being maybe 4 or 5 years old, and I hated *Don* Jacinto Orosco's voice on the radio."

Don Jacinto was a legendary disc jockey on a Spanish-language station who was known for his distinct, raspy voice.

"The only time I heard his voice was about 4:30 in the morning when we were on our way to Sahuarita to pick cotton on Saturday. This was in Dad's car. When my father could not go, and I was not in school, I would go with *Tía* Nala," Rudy recalls.

"When I went with her, we would go on a bus. I remember the stench.

"Hijo de su madre, como apestaba — el sudor. (Son of a bitch, how it smelled - the sweat). And this was going," he said, laughing.

Nala was still a master of stoop labor and continued beating some of the men, picking about 300 pounds a day and earning $40 a week.

While Nala worked in the fields, Tucson's southside lured more of the Bejarano and Téllez clan.

Nala's sister Florencia and her husband, Manuel Herrera, left Lordsburg, N.M., to begin a life here. The couple and their children, Raúl and Irene, moved into a travel trailer parked on brother Florentino's property at South 16th Avenue and West Michigan Street.

The Herreras later bought a trailer and lot on South 16th Avenue, just south of West Ajo Way, and Manuel went to work in the kitchen of the Veterans Administration Hospital.

Florencia applied for a nurse's aide position at hospitals and went to work in the fields alongside Nala while she waited.

Brother Florentino found a house for Mama Dolores, and she moved from Clifton into the house on West Michigan Street, near South Sixth Avenue.

Nala's younger brother, Juan, came with her, finding a job at Hughes Aircraft as a painter, a trade he learned in the Army.

Nala moved in with her mother and Juan.

The three-bedroom home would later shelter Nala's brother Isidro ("Chilo") and her sister Angela's grown children, Ambrosio and Natalia, who moved in with her husband, Freddy Peraza. (Natalia died in February 2013.)

The younger generations wanted more than cotton fields.

Before moving to Tucson, Chilo, Ambrosio, Freddy and Natalia lived in Benson, where the men worked at the Apache Powder Co. Ambrosio packed nitroglycerin for $2 an hour.

"We worked in small packing houses. The houses were covered with dirt so if there was an explosion not a lot of people died, only those in the house died. Before I began working there, three Mexican men died in an explosion in the mix house where nitroglycerin was handled."

"If a drop of nitro fell on the floor, I would get on my knees and start cleaning it with cotton right away. The floors were made of wood or lead," said Ambrosio.

Eventually, he and Chilo would get jobs at the mines, still handling explosives, drilling and blasting the tunnels at San Manuel.

It proved a wise choice. Unions were resurgent after the war. Job conditions and pay improved. The miners did much better for themselves and their families than their relatives who picked cotton.

In time, Ambrosio and Chilo moved their families to Tucson's northside. The subdivisions there were much different — nice middle-class homes in areas where Hispanic surnames were rare.

It was a time when parents pushed their children to learn English and forget Spanish because they needed to be American. It was a time when some lost their roots.

As the years passed, the families of the miners and the cotton pickers lost touch with each other.

Some moved to San Manuel and gave their lives to the underground, retiring after decades of hard, hard labor.

Last year, when San Manuel's mine shut down and the children and grandchildren of her brothers and sisters lost jobs, Mama started praying.

She prayed to God and Santa Elena de la Cruz that all the miners find new jobs.

In the 1950s, from Sahuarita to the south to Marana and beyond in the north, Nala's family toiled in the fields along the banks of the Santa Cruz, spanned by Interstate 19.
1994 Arizona Daily Star file photo.

While picking cotton in a field like this, Nala met Federico Duarte, her future husband.

Chapter 25: Daddy's demons

Daddy was a man with his share of troubles

While picking cotton at Midvale Farms, Mama met Federico Duarte, my Daddy.

Daddy was from the small mining town of La Colorada, Sonora. His mother, Carmen, had brought him and his two older brothers, Ricardo and Agustín, by wagon to Naco, Ariz., when they were young boys in 1914.

Among Grandma Carmen's possessions was a sewing machine. She worked as a seamstress to feed her boys. Agustín helped, laying railroad track in Naco at age 13.

The mother and sons eventually moved from Naco, following the seasonal crops in the farm fields of Pima and Pinal counties.

When Mama met Daddy in the fields at Midvale, Daddy had left a wife and five children behind in Eloy. He later divorced.

Daddy and Mama married and my brother, Raymond, was born at Tucson Medical Center in 1954. I was born there in 1956.

I loved Daddy and I felt very close to my paternal uncles, aunts and some of my cousins while growing up.

But when I grew older, I realized Mama suffered a lot because of Daddy. We all did.

Daddy appeared to be a happy-go-lucky fella, but he carried a demon. Mama's prayers to God and the *santos* didn't change that fact. Neither did my prayers.

I was 17 when my father died at Tucson Medical Center after a severe stroke.

Father George Reardon, then pastor at St. John the Evangelist Catholic Church, helped me let go of my father when the doctors told us that Daddy's brain was mush and he was breathing because of the machines attached to his body.

I remember Father Reardon telling me: "I'll be with him and administer last rites before they remove the machines. It will be all right."

That gave Mama and me so much comfort. Maybe hell wasn't in store for Daddy.

Daddy's death saddened me, but Mama and I also felt relief.

The story of my father is not one I can tell. Mama didn't ask for much, but she did beg her daughter, the journalist, not to tell it.

The journalist in me tried to change her mind, but lost.

Mama has had enough pain in her life. I will oblige her and tell the tale later, or maybe never.

For now, I'll just say that the life of Federico Duarte was richer for Mama's influence, even if her faith and prayers could not overcome his demons.

After my brother was born, Mama went to work in the mornings for a wealthy couple, Dan and Billie Liverman.

They lived in a white, ranch-style home just west of the Santa Cruz River, north of Ajo Way.

After she signed on with the Livermans, the county hospital finally offered her a job. Mama stayed on with Mrs. Liverman "because she had just hired me and I gave her my word."

That was important to Mama. Later, she realized she should have taken the county job. She could have worked her way up at the county, and she could have received benefits and a pension.

Mama earned $20 a week for working as a maid in the mornings. In the afternoons, she joined Daddy and other relatives in the fields. She paid her sister Florencia $5 a week to baby-sit Raymond.

Mama did not want more children. She couldn't afford them. When she got pregnant with me, she was tempted to give me away.

She and Daddy had just taken over the payments on the trailer and lot on South 16th Avenue where sister Florencia and her family had lived.

Florencia's family had moved to the house her mother, Dolores, was buying on Michigan Street after Dolores decided to return to Clifton.

Daddy, with the help of his brothers and their sons, built a two-room adobe house and moved the family from the trailer into the house. The toilet — with running water — was built in a room separate from the house. The family bathed in a washtub.

Mrs. Liverman knew Mama's situation. She wanted, but had been unable to have, children. She asked Mama to think about giving her the baby she had growing inside her.

"I will give the baby a good life, everything a child could want," she told Mama.

"We were so poor and I wondered about it," my Mama said today. "I told Federico, and he got angry. 'No, we are not giving away our baby.' "

Mama knew he was right, but she thought about everything her child would have with the Livermans — a beautiful house with indoor plumbing, nice clothes, travel, good schooling.

Fortunately, I was just too cute.

"When you were born, there was no way I could give you away. You were my baby, and I loved you," Mama tells me.

I first heard the story in fourth grade. I had eavesdropped at a window while she told Uncle Johnny's wife, *Nina* Eleanor, about her decision.

When *Nina* Eleanor left, I asked Mama through tears to explain why she didn't want me.

She hugged me tight and told the story over. She said I was one of God's most precious blessings in her life. I felt a little better, but it took time for all the hurt to go away.

After author Carmen Duarte was born, Nala decided to stay home and take in ironing. She made about $10 in a seven-day week, and the work took its toll in back pain. Photo by A.E. Araiza, Arizona Daily Star.

Chapter 26: My cousin's hell

Manuel the wife-beater was a 'mean, drunk marihuano'

After I was born in 1956, Mama decided to stay home and care for both her children at the home Daddy and his brothers had built on the south side.

"I wanted to raise you my own way. I wanted to teach you manners, morals and values. So I started ironing for others. I ironed clothes for four families, and I was paid about $10 a week. I ironed seven days a week, and my back hurt more from ironing than from picking cotton."

Daddy eventually left the fields and went to work cleaning south side bars before getting a job as a truck driver for a sand-and-gravel operation.

Life got better at our house. All worked. Raymond and I played in the dirt yards and streets, and everyone was healthy.

In the home of my Mama's sister, Florencia, and her husband, Manuel Herrera, things were different. Mama had been right about Manuel. He wasn't a nice man. He beat his wife viciously.

The women relatives knew, but when they tried to help Florencia leave, she defended him. She even resisted Mama, who pushed her to divorce him and leave with her children.

"She would tell me: 'He is my cross,' " Mama recalled. "They married through the Catholic Church, and the vows were important to Florencia. Police would arrest him, but she would not press charges.

"I would tell her, 'Let (brothers) Juan, Florentino and Chilo get ahold of him. Just let them know what he does to you. They'll make sure he doesn't do it again.' "

I think Mama could have done it herself. I saw my Daddy use physical force on her one time. He had been drinking. He came into the kitchen and grabbed her arm roughly. Mama picked up an iron skillet and whacked him in the head, just hard enough to get his attention.

"Touch me again and I'll kill you," she warned.

It worked on Daddy; Manuel Herrera was another story.

My cousins Jaime and Richard were too young to remember much, but Raúl and Irene still cannot forget those days, more than four decades ago.

"My father was mean, a drunk and a *marihuano*," said Raúl. "He was very macho, and his forte was always to have people on the edge of their seats.

"You never knew what he was going to do. He was a very unpredictable person. One minute he was OK. The next minute he was the devil.

"I was so small, but I would try to help my Mom so many times. I would jump on his back. I would kick him and bite him, whatever it took. I always got my ass whipped for it.

"I still have flashbacks of my Mom being on the bottom and him whipping on her. I'm all over his back. These are things that are very clear to me. ... I can never forget. It was rough."

Florencia had a second cross to bear. By 1958, she was seriously ill. The lymph nodes in her neck had swollen, as they had when she had tuberculosis in high school.

She went to the county hospital where she waited for hours to receive medical attention. You're poor, you take a number and wait. She got tired of waiting.

Florencia went home and kept getting weaker.

"I remember when they took my Mom to the hospital. She was almost in a coma," said Raúl, who was 11 at the time.

"She didn't even know who we were," said Irene, who was 9. "She was out of it. They took her in the ambulance. I didn't get to see her after she left."

Mama went to see Florencia. She had nursed her through tuberculosis. She had been so proud when Florencia graduated high school. She had expected, hoped for, prayed for, so much more for her little sister.

"I had to wear a gown and a mask, and could only stay minutes with her. She was pregnant. I prayed to *Santa Teresita de Jesús* to have God take her if she was to continue suffering. She had suffered enough."

Florencia died from meningitis just after Easter in 1958. The child she carried was too young to survive.

"I recall coming home from school and seeing my uncles' cars there," said Raúl.

"I knew something had happened. As soon as I walked into the house, I saw *Tía* (Nala). … There were a lot of people there. I saw their faces. I understood from their expressions that my Mom had passed away."

The news was delivered to Irene more harshly. "I remember walking home from school," she said, her voice cracking.

"The little boy across the street met me about three blocks from my house. He came up running and said, 'Irene, Irene, your mother died. Your mother died. Your mother's dead.'

"I ran all the way home. I remember my Uncle Johnny, my Aunt Eleanor and my Dad were there. They just sat me down and told me the news. It was just more bad things after that," she said.

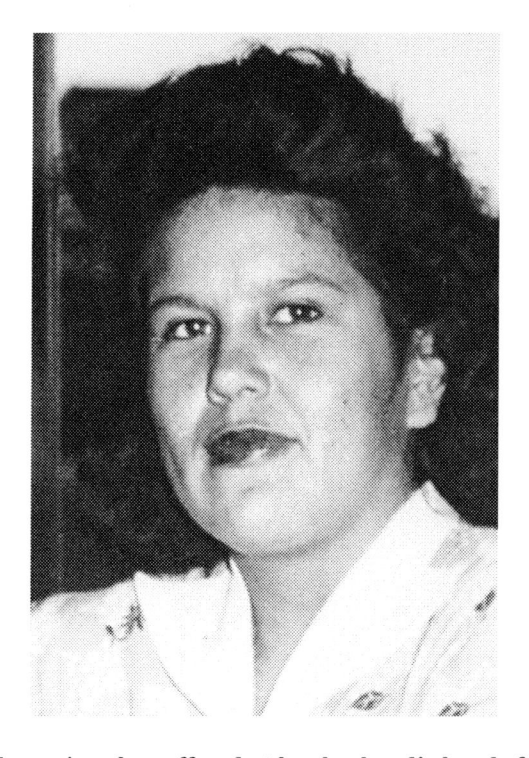

Nala's sister Florencia, who suffered at her husband's hands for many years, died of meningitis in 1958.

Raúl and Irene with parents Florencia and Manuel around 1951;
smiles hide a family in trouble

Chapter 27: The family doubles its size

Suffering cousins find 'la familia' at last

When Mama's sister Florencia died, my cousin Raúl was 11 years old. Irene was 9; Jaime, 4; and Richard, 3. Richard was at Comstock Children's Hospital in isolation because he had been born with tuberculosis.

Their father, Manuel, remarried soon after Florencia died, but the children continued to suffer.

He and his new wife neglected them. The cousins were often alone at the house on Michigan Street.

Sometimes there was no electricity, heat or running water. Sometimes, no food or clean clothes. And sometimes Raúl was beaten by his father.

The family was relieved when Manuel took three of his children to live with Grandma Dolores, who had moved to Clifton.

There, my cousins finally discovered *la familia*.

"My grandmother was very strict, but she was a good person," said Raúl.

"We had to go to Mass every morning, seven days a week.

"Little by little, I started understanding the word of God and about saying my prayers at night. I learned more from my grandmother than anyone about prayer.

"And every evening on bended knee, it was time to pray the rosary. I really never could figure out what the intention was," he said, laughing.

After morning Mass, Grandma made her grandchildren a good, hot breakfast. She paid a neighbor to take them to school and bring them home.

When not in school, Irene spent her time learning to knit, crochet and embroider. "Grandma did not believe in idle hands. We always had to be doing something," said Irene.

Raúl became close to our *Tía* Gumesinda, my Mama's oldest sister, who had stayed in nearby Morenci with her second husband, *Tío* Bernardo Vega, and their younger children.

"On the weekends, I would go stay with them up on the hill in Morenci," said Raúl.

"My *Tío* Benny was a great person. He was a person who never laid a hand on his kids. He would make them cry just by consulting with them, talking to them and telling them what they did wrong. It was worse than getting whipped," said Raúl.

Raúl, Irene and Jaime stayed for just one school year in Clifton. Their father, Manuel, came to take them back.

Grandma Dolores knew what was in store for her grandchildren. She left Clifton again and moved to a one-bedroom rental on West President Street, just south of West Ajo Way.

Soon enough, the Department of Public Welfare brought all four children to her.

By then, Richard had been released from Comstock Hospital.

He had been tied down to a bed for much of his first three years. He was quiet and withdrawn. He did not know his brothers, sister or grandma. *La familia* signified nothing. He would learn.

Dolores nourished the four and also baby-sat Raymond and me when we got older.

Mama had returned to the fields and did not like taking us with her in the winter.

It was in March 1961 that Manuel went to Grandma's house and terrorized her and his children once more.

He came at midnight. "He was yelling that he wanted me back," said Raúl. "Grandma got real sick from pure anger. I think that led to a lot of her health problems.

"I remember our neighbor, Mr. Rodríguez, came outside and told him to get the hell out of there." Oscar Rodríguez was a good neighbor. It was not the first time he had come to the rescue.

Soon after that, Grandma died.

I remember when it happened.

Mama was ironing and I was sitting nearby, feeling warm and safe as Mama pressed shirt after shirt.

There was a knock on the door, and my cousin Richard stood in the doorway with Oscar Rodríguez's sister-in-law, Rebecca. She had come to tell Mama that Grandma was very sick and calling for her.

Mama unplugged the iron, and we all walked to Grandma's house. Grandma was lying on the couch moaning and moaning.

She was taken to the county hospital where they operated on her. She suffered from kidney stones, and her intestines were blocked. Mama was with Grandma when she took her last, deep breath at the age of 72.

During the wake at Carrillo's Tucson Mortuary downtown, Grandma was dressed the way she had requested.

Tía Angela sewed her a replica of the white gown and blue robe worn in the statues that venerate Mary as the Immaculate Conception. Grandma was buried at Holy Hope Cemetery, not far from Florencia.

After the funeral, *Tía* Gumesinda stayed at Grandma's house with Raúl, Irene, Jaime and Richard.

Raymond and I stayed with Uncle Johnny and *Nina* Eleanor. Mama's strength had been waning. She thought she was pregnant again, but doctors had diagnosed a tumor shortly before Grandma died.

Mama went to Tucson Medical Center where she was prepared for surgery.

When Mama said goodbye to go to the hospital, she tried to look happy, but I felt something was wrong. I was scared that night, and *Nina* Eleanor hugged and comforted me while I cried myself to sleep.

God and the *santos* were with Mama once more. Doctor Hausmann removed a 9-pound benign tumor.

I was so happy when we returned to Grandma's house, which we would rent. It was only one bedroom, but it had indoor plumbing. *Tía* Gumesinda stayed with us for a while to help care for Mama.

Mama recovered quickly, and for a reason: She had decided that Florencia's four children would become her responsibility.

She did not want my cousins separated. My father said no. It would be impossible, financially. Mama stood her ground.

"They are my blood," Mama told him. "You are not. If you don't like it, you can leave."

Sammy Téllez and Rosie Alvarez accompany grandmother Dolores Téllez in downtown Tucson.

Author Carmen Duarte and her brother Raymond found a new world awaiting them when they moved from South 16th Avenue to their grandmother's house.

Chapter 28: Life with the cousins

8 people in a small house — and plenty of love for all

I don't remember much about moving from our two-room adobe house on South 16th Avenue to Grandma's one-bedroom house on West President in 1961.

But I do remember that indoor toilet, tub and shower. I thought that was great stuff. I was smart — even at age 5.

The house had a large porch and rosebushes in front.

Three orange trees with white blossoms perfumed the air, and lilies stretched along one end of the fence. Shade trees and a red oleander bush lined the other side of the yard.

In the back yard there was a large grapevine and apricot, apple, peach and pomegranate trees.

I have a vivid memory of sitting on a red velvet sofa in that house soon after moving in. I was watching television with Mama. She had her arm around me.

Then my younger cousins, Jaime and Richard, tried to nudge in. I remember clinging tightly to Mama and getting jealous. Mama laughed and hugged my cousins.

I learned Mama had enough love for all of us, and still some.

Good thing. There were wall-to-wall people in that house — eight of us. At night bodies stretched out everywhere — in the single bedroom, in the living room and in the kitchen.

At various times, I slept in Mama's bed, on the couch and on a rollaway bed. In summer, I would take my pillow and lie on the cement floor under the kitchen table. It was nice and cool.

I don't remember when I first saw my cousins as a part of me. All I know is that I grew to love them and they were my family.

The aroma of *chorizo con huevos, frijoles, papas* and *tortillas* awakened me on more mornings than I can remember.

It would be dark outside when Mama began making breakfast and lunches for all of us before we headed to the fields. On school days, of course, she headed to the fields and we did our jobs — getting an education.

On Mondays, Mama began her day at 2 a.m. because that was washday.

The Maytag wringer washer danced in the back yard as it cleaned pants, shirts, blouses, dresses and underwear.

The nine clotheslines that spanned the back yard were filled by the time Mama finished.

When we were preschool age, or during summer holidays and on Saturdays, we all headed out before sunup to hoe or pick cotton. During the summers, we cleared the fields of weeds. I did little of that because I suffered from severe allergies.

In the fall and winter, we picked cotton. We stood around campfires to keep warm until the dew dried on the cotton plants.

When the picking began, people talked about their lives and laughed. Others sang.

Cousin Jaime, of Buena Park, Calif., recalls those days: "*Tía* used to pick two rows of cotton. Raúl and Irene picked one row each, and you, Raymond, Richard and I would go ahead and pick cotton and leave piles so that they could put them in their sacks."

We earned enough money to eat, and Mama saved money to use toward buying clothes and shoes for us younger ones.

During the summer months, the older cousins, Raúl and Irene, worked 10-hour days, except on Saturday when the crews were off at noon.

Then they came home full of energy — ready to dance.

We little kids often entertained ourselves by watching Raúl and Irene get ready to go out.

Raúl would sing pop tunes — "The Twist," "Sherry" — as he ironed his khaki pants.

He had a good voice and played and sang in a band called The Nomads. But he'd make us laugh by singing high notes for the bass parts and vice versa.

Raúl was meticulous. His khakis had to have one sharp, straight crease down the middle of the pant leg. A double crease was deadly, and he would start over if one appeared.

Then he'd get the tin container of Shinola, and wax and spit, brush and buff until you could see your reflection in his black shoes.

Next came his jet-black hair. He rubbed in the hair cream and combed and combed until he had a perfect ducktail at the nape of his neck and a strand of hair falling just-so onto his forehead.

Irene had just as good a time, and it was fun seeing her and my cousin Rosie, who often visited from Morenci in summer, get dressed for their night out.

They'd put their hair up in pink and green rollers hours before.

The two would tease and wear their hair in a flip or French roll. They used tons of hair spray.

Before the dresses went on came the girdle race — my favorite part.

Irene and Rosie would pull and pull the elastic contraptions, howling as they reached their waistlines.

I remember I was in eighth grade when I wore my first girdle with stockings. It wasn't bad, but as I got older and wider … forget it.

I'd rather breathe than wear a tourniquet. What women go through to impress a man. Not this *chica*. I like food.

Heck, there are plenty of good men who love food, and I don't see them wearing girdles.

While my older cousins danced, Mama kept us four younger ones occupied at home playing poker for pennies and eating popcorn with Red Devil hot sauce.

Then we'd stay up late watching spooky movies on "Chiller."

We'd still have to wake up for 6 a.m. Mass at St. John's.

Sundays were special. We'd go on drives, hike in the desert or picnic in Madera Canyon.

Another Sunday favorite was visiting different churches in Southern Arizona.

Mama would go in and pray while we kids checked out the towns of Vail, Naco, St. David, Nogales and Douglas.

Irene and I laughed a lot and cried a lot remembering these times.

"Those are good memories, very good memories." Irene said.

Those are very good memories, my cousin, my sister.

It was so much fun, I didn't realize we were poor until I was much older.

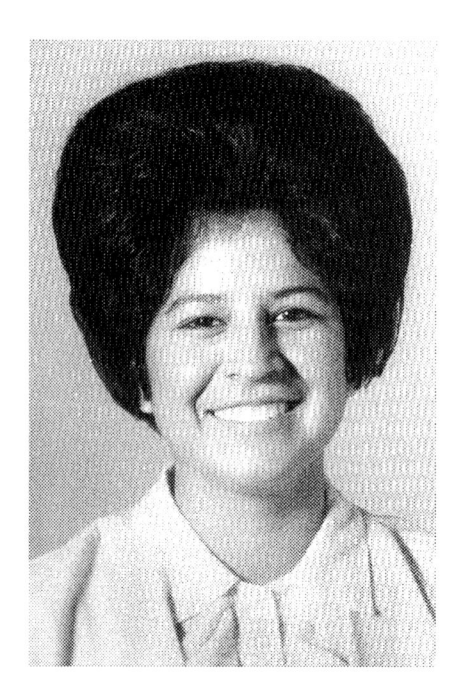

Hair rollers and oodles of spray were required before Irene
could go out for a good time on Saturday night.

Raúl, the sharp dresser, had absolutely no tolerance
for a less-than-perfect crease in his khakis.

Strangers flocked daily to Reyes' spacious yard, which includes a life-size sculpture of Jesus Christ on the cross. Reyes Ruiz, Tita's son, died in 2003. Photo by A.E. Araiza, Arizona Daily Star.

Chapter 29: Estela and *La Virgen*

Miracles happen, lives change when Blessed Mother speaks

Miracles happen daily in an impoverished barrio in South Phoenix where my cousin, Reyes Ruiz, has prayed his family into a life of service to the community and to *La Virgen*.

The family resisted for years.

His wife, Estela, considered Reyes an overly religious "lunatic" and was relieved when he went away on his pilgrimages in pursuit of his first love, the Blessed Mother.

One of his sons, state Sen. Armando Ruiz, was more interested in running for Congress than spreading the faith.

Another son, Rey Jr., was stoned on a variety of drugs when he wasn't driving an ambulance — and even when he was.

Then *La Virgen* spoke to Estela, and life has not been the same. It's been miraculously better.

Like my Mama's strong faith, Reyes' faith took root in the fertile valley of the Upper Gila River.

As a boy, Reyes would watch as his great-grandfather, Teófilo Bejarano, came from the fields to get a dipper of cool Gila River water from a wooden barrel.

Then Teófilo would kneel and pray, facing the picture of *La Virgen de Guadalupe* that hung from a barbed-wire fence, next to the one of *San Isidro*, the patron saint of farmers.

Reyes, whose mother, Tita, was my Mama's cousin and special friend as a girl in Virden, N.M., grew up in the knowledge that *La Virgen* and the *santos* were special.

So it was natural that, at age 7, he turned to the Blessed Mother for comfort when he lost his father, Ysidoro.

Ysidoro, Tita's first husband, died after being struck by a pickup truck one winter morning while walking with fellow *campesinos* to clean out irrigation ditches for the *patrones* in Virden.

The driver of the truck had cleared a small section of early morning frost from the windshield. He did not see the men walking by the side of the road. The truck plowed into Ysidoro. It was 1940, and Reyes was in first grade at Virden School. "They came after me," said Reyes from his south side Phoenix home, a home whose yard has been converted into a shrine dedicated to Our Lady of the Americas.

His mother and other relatives met up with the young boy who was running toward home after hearing the news about his father.

All headed for the doctor's office in Virden. The pickup truck, with Ysidoro in the bed, was leaving, headed for the hospital in Lordsburg.

"It was very painful to see my mother crying. She was very emotional," said Reyes.

When Ysidoro died, Reyes wanted to be strong for his mother.

He wanted to carry the cross in front of the procession leading to the family's cemetery near Tita's and *Nana* Leonarda's homes.

"I couldn't carry it. I put it down and let somebody else take it. I went and grabbed my Mom's hand. In grabbing her hand and looking for consolation, I saw there was none because she (Tita) was hurting. I was very upset at God. He was the one responsible for taking my father. I was angry at him for a long time.

"In being mad at God, I think that one of the most beautiful things that happened was that I found this beautiful lady that was loved very much by all my family. This beautiful lady was our Blessed Mother. I knew I needed this love.

"I would see my family praying in front of her picture, in front of the altar or just in quietness. By the time I was 13 years of age, I was a young man that was totally in love with her," said Reyes.

That devotion has spread.

La Virgen has changed Estela and the couple's six children — Isidoro, twins Armando and Fernando, Rey, Rosie and Rebecca. She also has touched a seventh child, Tony, the son of neighbors, who entered the family's home as a toddler and never left.

The changes began while Reyes was on a pilgrimage in 1988 to Medjugorje, a farming and sheep-herding village in western Bosnia that is home to mostly Roman Catholic Croatians.

Reyes had moved from Safford to Phoenix in 1957 and helped build the metropolis as a bricklayer and later a masonry contractor.

After his firm went bankrupt in the mid-1970s during a building recession, Reyes began working for the Roman Catholic Diocese of Phoenix, bringing God to migrant farmworkers.

He ministered in the citrus groves and brought priests to say Mass to the *campesinos*.

He also gave workshops to FBI agents about abuses suffered by undocumented workers, and helped uncover cases of outright slavery in Arizona.

On a trip to Boston in the late 1980s to give a report about the plight of the farmworkers to the church's national Office of Hispanic Affairs, Reyes found out that *La Virgen* had been appearing in Medjugorje since 1981.

His love for her and his hopes to save his family took him to the mountainous hamlet where countless sightings of *La Virgen* were reported by pilgrims who traveled from all parts of the world to see her.

There, in St. James Church, Reyes prayed for Estela and his children. As he prayed, Reyes said, he was overtaken by a deep sense of peace that could only come from God.

He prayed for his family to find God, to truly do God's work and become saints.

He prayed for them to escape the worldly trap they were in:

• Estela was a devoted wife and mother, who returned to school at Reyes' urging after her children were grown.

She received her bachelor's degree and enrolled in a master's program at Northern Arizona University while working for the Murphy School District as director for bilingual education. She was a woman on the move.

• Twins Armando and Fernando, both Loyola Marymount University graduates, were concerned only with their careers.

Armando had been elected as a state representative in 1982.

Fernando was an insurance underwriter who ran Armando's political campaigns.

• Rosie was in banking.

• Rebecca was an educator.

• Isidoro, also a Loyola Marymount graduate, works for the Los Angeles County judicial system.

• Rey was an ambulance driver, drug addict and drug pusher who toyed with death. He was living la *vida loca*, haunted by the devil.

While Reyes was in Medjugorje, climbing hills and praying for his family, Estela was happy for the respite from her "holy roller" husband.

She had grown tired of him trying to persuade her to go to Mass, receive the Holy Eucharist and pray the rosary daily.

But Estela only thought she was free of Reyes' pestering.

On her way to the kitchen to put on a pot of coffee early one morning, Estela had to pass through the living room, which Reyes had converted into a shrine to La Virgen de Guadalupe.

As she passed a picture of *La Virgen*, she heard a voice — a woman's voice.

"Good morning, daughter."

She decided not to believe her ears.

Days later, it happened again.

"Good morning, daughter."

This time Estela answered. "Good morning, Blessed Mother."

Now she was stuck. There was no way to take back the words. Reyes is crazy, she thought, and now it's her turn.

She kept it her little secret.

When Reyes returned to South Phoenix in September 1988, Estela noticed a change in her husband. There was an aura about him.

He was rejuvenated by his trip, and the family couldn't help but listen when he spoke about the Croatian village and his sense of God's profound peace and the presence of *La Virgen*.

The family began gathering to pray the rosary, and Estela found herself accompanying her husband to daily Mass.

In December, *La Virgen* appeared to Estela as she prayed the rosary in her bedroom, along with her husband, her son Fernando, and Fernando's wife, Leticia.

"The beautiful lady" with piercing blue eyes appeared and told Estela she would take care of her children.

Days later, *La Virgen* appeared to Estela in the living room of her home and asked her to be her messenger.

Estela accepted the call. Since then, *La Virgen* has appeared to Estela hundreds of times, giving her messages of love from God.

The messages are simple and easily summed up in the manner Jesus does in the gospels: Love God and love one another; all else will take care of itself.

At first, the Ruiz family kept the apparitions to themselves.

"That first year was pure enjoyment with her," said Estela. "She was all ours. But, of course, that was when she was working with us. She was knocking sense into our heads because of our muleheadedness."

Daughter Rebecca said: "We prayed, and she gave us many blessings. Family members would cry and say, 'I saw her.' We would call her appearances candy kisses."

"It was during this time that she was winning our hearts over," Estela said.

Son Rey, the gangbanger with the drug-crazed lifestyle, said he gave a message to *La Virgen*: "Well, you take me the way I am, or leave me alone."

"Our Lady came to Mom and said, 'Tell him that's the way I want him. I don't ask any change of him,' " said Rey.

"After I was told that, it was basically my choice to say yes or no. Once I said yes, that's when the change started. Our Lady was the inspiration in changing my life, and many other people who were on drugs, too."

Son Armando believed his mother. He thought the apparitions were wonderful.

"That was my first response. My second response was, 'I'm up for re-election. How is this going to impact me?' " he said, belting out a contagious laugh.

Armando served from 1982 to 1990 in the House, and then two more years as a state senator. He worried that his mother's spirituality would interfere with his public life.

"Even though God inspires you, you still have those things of the world. You are still grounded in the world, and I had a very natural reaction. Are people going to think my mom's nuts? Are they going to think I'm nuts? Will they still vote for me?"

The voters didn't seem to mind. Armando was re-elected, and in 1992 he had his sights set on Congress.

The state Senate had a Democratic majority, and he wanted to draw himself a Democratic congressional seat through redistricting.

But first he went on a junket to Mexico City with other state officials.

The group toured the Basílica de La Virgen de Guadalupe.

Armando recalls standing on the conveyor belt that took him to the image of the Blessed Mother on the *tilma* that Juan Diego wore centuries ago.

He stepped off the conveyor to pray before the image.

"I was in front of her for at least five minutes. I felt very much her presence, and I felt her stirring in my heart. I walked away from there convinced that I was meant to run for Congress. She was calling me to greater power, to enjoy the fruits of the world," he said.

"I came back and started to put the exploratory committee together. I started to carve out the congressional district that I wanted."

But something nagged at Armando.

"It was during Lent, and I continued to pray. One evening, I remember telling my wife, 'Maybe God is calling me to something very, very different. Maybe I've really missed the boat with this. Maybe God is asking me to leave this, not because politics is bad, but because politics was my god.' "

"It came first before everything else. I lost several families because of it," said Armando, who is in his third marriage.

Armando decided not to run.

"I called the people who were helping me and said, 'I love politics. I enjoy it. I think it's a wonderful thing that people can do. But God is calling me on a different road right now.' "

"People were just shocked. They were shocked that I would walk away from the hustle and bustle of politics for something obscure, something about God."

His good friends and political allies respected his decision: Democratic Sens. Pete Rios and Jaime Gutiérrez; House Minority Leader Art Hamilton, his mentor and godfather to one of his children; even Republican Gov. Fife Symington.

Armando was proud of some things he had done in office. He helped reverse the state's English-only act. He worked on neighborhood revitalization projects, worked with troubled barrio youths.

But now he is doing more, and none of it for political gain.

In December, as Armando talked to me about his new calling, about 100 people from around the world were at the family home, attending Mary's Ministries 11th Annual Retreat, a spiritual rejuvenation gathering for evangelical lay workers, priests and nuns.

They came for spiritual rejuvenation before the shrine to Our Lady of the Americas that the Virgin asked Reyes to build 12 years ago.

Strangers flock daily to the spacious yard landscaped with grass, trees and vibrant red, yellow and purple flowers.

Reyes has sculpted life-size statues, including Jesus Christ on the cross. The wood came from a tree at the Perryville prison. Christ's head of hair comes from a woman and child who lost it during cancer treatments, and the beard once belonged to Reyes.

For years, when *La Virgen* gave public messages through Estela, hundreds crowded into the yard to hear.

Now, *La Virgen* gives only personal messages to the family. The messages give them strength and direction to do God's work, said Estela.

All have been changed.

Rey walked away from dealing and using drugs.

Armando left politics.

Fernando, Isidoro, Rebecca, Rosie and Tony all began praying for answers and working for God.

The family has become nationally known. "For the Soul of the Family," a book written by Thomas W. Petrisko, tells the story of the apparitions to Estela. Reyes and Estela appeared on "Geraldo," "The Joan Rivers Show," NBC's "Prophecies" and "The Sally Jessy Raphael Show."

Reyes and Estela traveled for 10 years evangelizing. Now nearly all their children have taken up the calling.

The family founded an evangelical school. "We have a community of people that work with us, and they go out all over the world," said Estela.

While evangelizing in Peru in 1999, Rey picked up a virus that caused him to lose his eyesight. He slowly regained it, and as soon as he could, Rey hit the road again as God's warrior.

In 1994, the family opened a charter school, adjacent to Estela and Reyes' home. It offers a college preparatory curriculum.

It has an enrollment of nearly 700 students in preschool through high school.

"The reason we started it was because of what was going on here in our community. The kids were killing each other. Kids had no respect for anybody. I was disenchanted," recalls Estela.

Now the youth of South Phoenix are learning respect and values, along with reading, writing and arithmetic, Estela said.

In 1996, the school was awarded $1 million by the National Football League. The money bought 35 computers, a radio station and a television station, classrooms and a multipurpose room.

A second charter school has opened in the Gila River Valley, in Safford. Relatives who saw what the Ruiz family had done in South Phoenix work at the school.

The family also is involved in neighborhood development.

Espíritu is a nonprofit agency with a $5 million annual budget that operates the programs. It also helps families buy their own homes and improve their neighborhoods.

Armando is the chief executive officer.

Mary's Ministries is the second non-profit group and deals with worldwide evangelization and spiritual leadership development, said Armando. Its annual budget is $200,000.

"God gives you talent as a community of people. God moves you in your heart to take the talents he's given you and make a contribution to the world. I really am happy. God gives you peace. He gives you purpose," said Armando, his face radiating.

I ask cousin Reyes and Estela: "Anyone in your family become a saint yet?"

Both look at each other and break out in laughter.

"It's a lifetime work," said Estela.

Reyes pauses: "I believe that some of my ancestors are saints. Their prayers were very, very powerful."

Those are my ancestors as well. Perhaps the *santos* are closer than I thought.

Reyes, who died in 2003, and Estela Ruiz address participants
in the 11th annual retreat of Mary's Ministries.

How La Virgen appeared to Juan Diego

On Dec. 9, 1531, Juan Diego was on his way to Mass. The campesino was walking through the desert on the outskirts of Mexico City.

He heard a voice as he approached Tepeyac Hill.

"Juan, where are you going?" asked the voice. Juan ran up the hill and saw a glowing figure of a beautiful lady. He dropped to his knees. "I'm going to Mass," he answered.

The beautiful, dark-skinned woman told Juan to go see the bishop of Mexico City and tell him that she wanted a church built in her honor on the hill.

Juan obeyed and spoke to Bishop Juan Zumárraga. He told the educated man his story, and Zumárraga did not believe it. The hill once was home to a pagan temple. He told Juan that he would reflect on what he had told him.

On his way home Juan passed by Tepeyac Hill, where *La Virgen* was waiting for him. Juan apologized to *La Virgen*, saying he had done his best. He asked her to send someone more important to do her work.

La Virgen told him to return the next day. Juan obediently went and spoke to the bishop again, repeating *La Virgen*'s request.

Zumarraga asked Juan for a sign from *La Virgen*.

Juan returned to the hill and told La Virgen that the bishop wanted a sign. La Virgen told her faithful servant to return the following day.

The next day Juan was torn between going to see the beautiful lady and going to church to find a priest for his sick, dying uncle.

He took a different route to church, but *La Virgen* appeared to him there as well.

Juan was embarrassed and ashamed for avoiding her. He explained why he had not met her. She lovingly told him: "Do not worry about your uncle's illness. He is not to die."

Then she told Juan to go to the top of the hill and gather flowers. It was a cold winter, but he found a variety of colorful roses.

He picked the roses and gathered them inside his *tilma*, or cloak.

Juan went to the bishop, and when he opened his *tilma* the flowers fell to the floor. On the *tilma* was the image of *La Virgen* de Guadalupe.

The bishop fell to his knees and immediately began planning to build a church in *La Virgen's* honor.

La Virgen's feast day is celebrated Dec. 12. Juan Diego's *tilma*, which has undergone scientific studies, hangs in the *Basílica de La Virgen de Guadalupe* in Mexico City.

Scientists cannot explain how the *tilma* has lasted so long without the fibers disintegrating, said the Rev. Raúl Trevizo, pastor of St. John the Evangelist Catholic Church

Chapter 30: The 1960s

War tested a family's faith, opened horizons

The military was one route from poverty for my patriotic cousins.

That made the 1960s a time of great stress for *la familia*. My cousins went off to war early in the Vietnam era and served multiple tours.

Mama was praying to *Nuestra Señora de la Victoria* (Our Lady of Victory) long before much of the nation had recognized the seriousness of our involvement.

My cousin Jaime, one of the cousins Mama helped raise, quit high school in 1970, joined the Army and volunteered for Vietnam. Mama prayed for the Army to say no. She thought the family had already sent enough sons to Southeast Asia.

Rudy Bejarano was sent to Vietnam in the early days of the war. Bejarano was hit by shrapnel while he was on patrol; many in his brigade were killed.
Photo courtesy of Rudy Bejarano.

Two of her brother Florentino's sons, Rudy and Floyd Bejarano, had already served their tours by then. Her sister Gumesinda's boys, Lalo and Domingo Vega, went as well.

Rudy Bejarano was a Pueblo High graduate who had dreamed of attending a military academyut he was a poor Hispanic teen with no political ties. Instead, he enrolled at the University of Arizona and joined ROTC. He volunteered for active duty before graduation and served his first tour in Vietnam in 1967.

There he found religion.

Rudy let out a long sigh and hesitantly recalled the bloody war that he said the United States lost because politicians did not let soldiers do their jobs.

And that, he said, cost many American lives.

"The first year I was with the 173rd Airborne Brigade, a U.S. combat infantry unit. I did my job, and I'd like to think that I did a good job in terms of being an infantry platoon leader, a company exec and, for a short time, a company commander.

"I got to Vietnam approximately Oct. 10, 1967, and on Nov. 13 we went into Dak To, near the border with Cambodia and Thailand. We got our ass kicked.

"The 173rd Airborne Brigade had four battalions. The whole brigade is about 3,000 people, actual combat people vs. support people.

"The officer corps — about 60 percent were wounded or killed. The enlisted - troops if you will — probably about 50 percent were killed or wounded."

Rudy was one of the casualties — hit by shrapnel. "There was one good-size piece in my leg. The rest were minor.

"The reason I got religion, and to this day I know that was the critical thing in my life, was having been wounded and just lying there, waiting to be evacuated, and one of our own planes, not a jet but an A-5, came over low."

It dropped a bomb.

"The bomb was a 500-pound bomb, a huge bomb. It landed, see that *mueble*, right over there," he said, pointing to his living room sofa.

"It landed that far from me. I saw it fall. Bang. The huge thump. The ground shook. I thought, 'We're gone.'

"But it didn't explode. It gives you religion. It gives you religion."

That same day, after Rudy had been evacuated, his platoon staged an assault on a target called Hill 875. Most didn't survive.

"It was not my turn to go. That's where I got religion."

Rudy recovered from the shrapnel wound in his leg and was sent back to the battlefield two weeks later. He also survived front-line duty in the Tet Offensive of 1968 and came home with a Purple Heart, three Bronze Stars and an Air Medal, among other commendations.

He and his brother Floyd and his cousins Lalo and Domingo all came home.

Rudy found the military to be a good step for a poor kid from the southside. The Army helped him finish college.

He retired from the Army Reserve as a lieutenant colonel and later served two terms as a Tucson city councilman. He and his wife, his high school sweetheart Esperanza, have a nice home on the westside, north of St. Mary's Hospital, where they have raised four children.

Esperanza is a retired school teacher and principal.

Rudy has his own accounting business, and he and Esperanza renovated Esperanza's family home in Sonoyta, Sonora, and turned it into a school where they go on weekends to teach English to Mexican children. They call their program *Esperanza en el Ingles* (Hope in English).

The real family tragedy in the '60s was the stabbing death of Mama's brother Isidro, *Tío* Chilo.

Tío Chilo would show up at our house on rainy Saturdays and most Sunday mornings to chat with Mama as she cooked breakfast and piled fresh-made *tortillas* into a stack on a clean dish towel on the kitchen table. We kids would empty the stack almost as fast as she built it.

Chilo was a short, stocky man who always wore jeans, a white shirt, a cowboy hat and a big smile.

After the hellos, he'd get a tall glass, pour tomato juice, crack a raw egg into the glass, pour in Red Devil hot sauce, sprinkle salt and pepper and stir up the drink.

He'd bring the glass to his lips and swallow until the liquid disappeared. Sometimes Daddy would join him with his own glass.

Later, I found out this helped some beat a hangover. I tried it when I was much, much older, but it really didn't help me.

Tío Chilo was close to Mama. They'd talk about anything and everything. She was his confidante. When he was stabbed to death in 1966 by his stepdaughter, the entire family was numbed.

I rarely have seen Mama cry. She cried for Chilo.

Mama prayed to Our Lady of Mount Carmel, her attorney for the dead, to intercede on Chilo's behalf and ask God to grant him an entrance to heaven.

Tío Chilo's stepdaughter was 16 at the time. Convicted of his death, she served time until she was an adult.

Chilo's death and the murder trial with its accusations and defenses, caused a large tear in the fabric of *la familia* that is still being slowly repaired.

Tucsonans Rudy Bejarano and wife, Esperanza, opened a weekend school in Sonoyta, Sonora. In the thick of the Vietnam War, soldier Rudy found new faith after a brush with death. Photo by A.E. Araiza, Arizona Daily Star.

Carmen Duarte returns to the rectory of St. John the Evangelist, where she worked for $1 an hour as an eighth grader. Photo by A.E. Araiza, Arizona Daily Star.

Chapter 31: From picker to maid
Mama found ways to beat poverty

By the time I was in seventh grade in 1968, the cotton-picking machines had taken over the fields.

At age 50, Mama searched for a new occupation.

Tucson's face was changing. Subdivisions and shopping centers sprouted and eventually gobbled up the farm fields where barrio families had long labored to eke out a life.

Picking was Mama's life. She had grown up doing it, and I don't think she ever figured she deserved better.

It was difficult for her to imagine a better job, since she could not read or write well.

She felt like *la burra*, the beast of burden, who did the sweaty jobs for others who made her feel inferior.

Mama's *pollitos* inherited some of those insecurities.

I remember having to fight off those thoughts in high school. I was ashamed of being poor, and I felt inferior around those who were financially better off.

Mama never wanted our friends to come to our house. We were too poor, she'd say.

"If friends came over, they had to sit outside," my cousin Raúl recalls. "If they wanted to go to the bathroom, tough. (We said) there was no bathroom here," he said, laughing.

I shouldn't have cared. The barrio was full of poor *compadres* and *comadres*. Maybe some were better off than us, but they knew poverty, too. I can laugh about it now, but back then it did a whole number on my psyche.

I was angry about being poor, and poor Mama bore the brunt of my anger.

I can't count the times I told her that I should have never been born. Mama just put her head down and prayed to God and her *santos*.

He had given her the strength to survive this life. Certainly he would give her strength to survive six teen-agers — their mouths and their moods.

Mama, meanwhile, found work as a maid at the Pickwick Motel on Benson Highway.

She walked to and from the motel, worked hard and left rooms spotless. She earned $1 an hour, some weeks making less than in the fields.

(Next time you stay at a motel, for God's sake leave the maids a generous tip.)

But Mama had a knack for managing what little money the family had. She also had a knack for making great meals from government surplus food.

After we took in my cousins Raúl, Irene, Jaime and Richard, the social workers told Mama to go each month to a building west of North Fourth Avenue, not far from the railroad tracks, to get the family's allotment of food.

We stood in line with the other poor families. We came home with rice, powdered milk and eggs, peas, white beans, blocks of cheese, peanut butter and canned meat.

The canned meat was similar to corned beef, and Mama would make *chorizo* with it, using Mogen David wine and red chile. Sounds odd, I know, but it was delicious.

Mama also made the fluffiest scrambled eggs from the powder, mixing in *papas*, *tomate* and *chile verde*.

She had the most trouble getting us to drink the milk.

"There are hungry people in the world," Mama would say. "Don't waste food. God will punish you for being wasteful."

Yes, Mama. She brainwashed me, and that's why to this day I usually clean my plate, even when I'm stuffed.

We thanked God for Nestle's Quik chocolate and strawberry flavors to help the milk go down.

In eighth grade, I got a job.

Sister Esther Marie, a wonderful teacher at St. John the Evangelist School, asked me one day if I would like to work as a receptionist on Saturday at St. John's rectory.

I talked it over with Mama and I went to work. At age 13, I earned the same $1 an hour Mama made.

I began each Saturday at 8 a.m. and brought home $8 a week. Mama let me keep the money, and I learned to save and buy clothes.

When I went to Pueblo High School, my rectory job helped me through business courses. I practiced my typing on letters for the priests and filling out baptismal, confirmation and marriage certificates.

On Sundays and in the summers, I went to help Mama at the motel, which changed names over the years to Sage & Sand and The Lazy 8.

She'd make the beds and clean the bathrooms, while I dusted, vacuumed and emptied the trash. I'd come home with aching muscles and wonder about Mama's strength. It was not of this world.

Mama could have gotten rich at the job if she were more felonious.

Tucson has long been a gateway for drug activity, and Mama would find the leftovers — guns, cocaine, marijuana and money.

She just turned it all in to the manager. Once, she forgot and came home with a bag of white powder in her dress pocket.

I freaked. I could picture my poor Mama getting busted.

Mama laughed and brushed my fears aside. "Don't worry," she said, and flushed the powder down the toilet. She seemed to always know what to do.

As we grew, we kids pitched in more and more. I worked at the rectory. Cousin Jaime became a bag boy at the Lucky supermarket at Southgate Shopping Center. My brother Raymond worked at the Dairy Queen on South 12th Avenue, and cousin Richard made the football team.

Mama kept reminding us to do well in school and graduate.

It was too late for teen-agers Raúl and Irene. They had already quit school, married and left the home on West President Street.

Irene believes God sent George Romero and his parents, Altagracia and Alejandro, into her life.

Chapter 32: Raúl and Irene

Two tough beginnings, two happy endings

The lives of my cousins Raúl and Irene started out tough. But both are crafting happy endings for themselves.

Raúl began to feel more secure after he, Irene, Jaime and Richard squeezed into my family's one-bedroom home.

Familia — that feeling of belonging he first found in his short stays with Grandma Dolores — grew under Mama's care.

And even when he was basically on his own, he did well in school — and he loved sports.

"Sports took me off a road to ruin," he said.

"When we moved back to Tucson, and I lived with my father, I hung around with a gang. We used to steal.

"I was looking for something. My father was very abusive.

"Sometimes I would not see him for a week or two. I'd wash my own clothes and make my own food. I just survived."

Raúl made the all-city football team at Wakefield Junior High. At Pueblo High School, he learned more discipline under Coach Lou Farber.

"He and Ed Brown, an assistant coach, were very instrumental in my life. They were very good people and role models."

Raúl was becoming a star at running back and linebacker.

Then at age 16, he became a father. Belen, his high school sweetheart, gave birth to a boy, David.

The couple married shortly before Raúl turned 17, and moved into a house off South 10th Avenue in the City of South Tucson.

In his junior year, a knee injury ended his football career. Worse, he couldn't work for a while.

The good news was that a larger community beyond his family cared for him.

The student body, faculty and coaches hosted fund-raisers to help the young couple.

Dan Eckstrom, later mayor of South Tucson and after that, a Pima County supervisor, sold tamales his mother made to raise money.

"There are not enough words to express what Dan and the officers, coaches and students did for me. They were great people," said Raúl.

Raúl quit school and went to work — bag boy, stock clerk, foreman at a manufacturing plant.

He bought his first house, a four-bedroom home, in 1975.

That year he and Belen had their fourth child, Celina. Their two other sons are Greg and Steve. Raúl continued to work hard, usually holding two jobs, and in the 1980s he bought his dream home — a two-story, four-bedroom house in a southwest subdivision close to lush desert hills.

"It was a house that I wanted all my life. But, you know, having what you want and being unhappy just doesn't work. We ended our marriage there."

Raúl remarried in 1989. His wife, Mary, is a petite woman with a kind heart.

If Raúl had his life to live over, he would wait on marriage, continue his education and emphasize education to his children.

But he thanks God the kids turned out well, and he's pushing college for his eight grandchildren.

He also thanks God for Mama.

"I used to always say the Lord has taken a lot away from me. He took my mother, my grandmother. But, I realized, he blessed me with my aunt. So he really never took anything away from me."

Irene dropped out of school in 1964 to marry Reynaldo Martinez, a handsome, muscular man she met while dancing at Del Rio ballroom. She was 16; he was 18.

"When we first married, Rey used to work in cotton. When the cotton season was over at the end of December, we went to California. There were beets, grapes, potatoes, tomatoes and oranges.

"I worked with a lot of pesticides. Pilots would spray the fields by plane, and we'd be working there," said Irene, who a year later gave birth to a son.

"We didn't stay too long the following year because Little Ray kept getting sick.

They came back to Marana and chopped lettuce in the fields.

"Oh, God, it was a lot of stoop labor with the short hoe. We'd be bent for hours and hours and hours."

Irene got pregnant again, giving birth to Tina Louise in 1966.

And Rey turned out to be unfaithful and violent. Irene had seen her mother suffer such a relationship. She would not.

They separated. Irene picked lettuce up to 12 hours a day, seven days a week, while a friend cared for her children.

Her divorce was final in 1970. By then, the single mother had met George Romero.

She believes God sent him and his parents into her life.

George's parents, Altagracia and Alejandro Romero, had left the ranches and fields for South Tucson where Alejandro built and maintained the city's streets.

Altagracia made Irene her project. "Come to Tucson and get a job. Go to school. You have to do something with your life to better yourself," she told her.

When the Welfare Department offered her an opportunity to go to school, she went for it.

She moved into a trailer park on Tucson's south side with her children. She enrolled in a job-training program and became a nurse's aide, following in her mother, Florencia's, footsteps.

In 1971, Irene began working at St. Mary's Hospital rehabilitation unit with stroke patients and others who suffered from paralysis and brain injuries.

She and George were married in 1972. George, an insurance agent, moved his family into a nice southwest-side mobile home park, on the site of retired cotton fields along South Mission Road.

Irene gave birth to Gracie in 1973, and later went to work as an assembly worker at various electronics plants before returning to work with the elderly.

She suffers from numerous illnesses including fibromyalgia, a muscle disorder that causes agonizing pain and inflammation.

But she still wakes each day with a good morning first to God, the Blessed Mother and the *santos*.

Irene and George keep *la familia* together, hosting all the family celebrations.

George is the king of *carne asada*.

The cookouts are mostly an excuse to gather everyone together with Mama to play poker.

Every time Mama walks into her home, Irene just smiles.

Even when Raúl was basically on his own he did well in school, and, "Sports took me off a road to ruin," he said.

Life has been a drug roller coaster for Richard; he kicked his habit in high school, graduated and later went back to drugs, but he's clean now. Photo by A.E. Araiza, Arizona Daily Star.

Chapter 33: Jaime and Richard

Long hair? No problem; drugs? Yes, problem

In the late 1960s and early '70s, Mama suddenly found herself with a house full of hippies.

Jaime was first. Once he no longer had to wear parochial school uniforms, he blended with the other teens at Pueblo High School who dressed in torn jeans and T-shirts and grew their hair long below the ear.

Richard got into the scene in the early 1970s.

My brother Raymond never grew his hair long.

The furthest I got was wearing jeans, boots and my old, faithful blue knitted poncho. I parted my long, black, straight hair down the middle and listened to a lot of Carole King and Santana with my sidekick, Aida. Man, we were cool.

Mama took it all in stride, so long as it was simply a fashion statement and we continued to bring home good grades.

What bothered her was drugs. She prayed to *Santo Niño de Atocha* to keep us straight.

Jaime was first to smoke pot.

"I prayed and told him that being a *marihuano* was not good. He was too big to spank. All I could do was talk to him," Mama said.

Jaime seemed to settle down.

"I was glad. Jaime was very intelligent. He just had to learn to use his intelligence," said Mama.

She kept praying for her nephew, whom she lovingly called *"cabezón,"* blockhead.

"*Tía* is the ultimate mother and aunt," said Jaime. "Even though my childhood was troubled, it wasn't from her. She was always good to us. All my inner trouble was caused by memories of my dad."

When Jaime reached his senior year, he wanted to quit school and join the Army.

El cabezón would not listen to Mama: "Graduate from high school first."

"He told me he would finish high school in the service.

"Jaime was the adventurer. He did what popped into his mind. And he was always laughing. That was his personality. You could be scolding him and he was smiling."

The Army was not the best place for a budding *marihuano*. San Francisco was not the ideal posting; neither was Germany.

"I got into a lot of different types of drugs. I took LSD, acid, cocaine, speed, downers and I smoked a lot of hash. There was a lot of drugs being done all over. It was so easy to get drugs there," he recalls.

Jaime was lucky he never got hooked on drugs.

Maybe the prayers worked.

Jaime came home after the Army, but didn't stay long.

He went out to a nightclub one night and never returned.

Then he finally telephoned. He was in Los Angeles. He had gone for the weekend, but had decided to stay. He's still there.

Jaime married and had three children with wife, Rita.

Edelle is a chiropractic assistant; Krystal is a baker; and James is a sheriff's deputy. Jaime and Rita were married for 17 years before they divorced.

In 1996, Jaime married Shelly, a single mother with a 12-year-old daughter.

Richard went through drastic changes in high school. He was a clean-cut football player his freshman year, as his big brother Raúl had been in the 1960s.

But Richard's life took a turn when he discovered drugs his sophomore year.

The long, long hair and tattered jeans were just a symptom.

Mama began praying again to God and *Santo Niño de Atocha* to show Richard the light. She knew way before anyone else where Richard was headed, but he did not heed her *consejos*.

"I left sports and fell behind in my classes, dropping out my sophomore year," recalls Richard.

"I did a lot of pot, LSD, mescaline and a lot of speed. I tried heroin once. I sniffed it, but I didn't like it. I never did it again. Once, my *Tía* found a bag of marijuana in my (dresser) drawer. I was busted. She flushed it down the toilet."

It just took time before he was arrested. He ended up at Pima County Juvenile Detention Center. Richard had a choice: face lockup or go back to school and straighten out.

He chose school, and Mama lighted another candle.

Richard had to repeat his sophomore year, and he needed to show Pueblo High football coaches Don Bowerman and Bill Bell he meant business before he was allowed to play football.

He cut his hair and got back into shape.

"This training taught me a lot of discipline, mentally and physically. It taught me that there are two sides to your body. You can either take care of it, or let it go to crap like I did. I felt the before and the after. I lost weight, and I got all that crap out of me," said Richard, who now works long days as a plumber in the new subdivisions sprouting in metropolitan Tucson.

At Pueblo High, Richard played defensive tackle and aspired to be a star his senior year like his older brother Raúl. But his experience was too much like Raúl's.

His playing time abruptly ended when he injured his leg. The injury did win him votes for Homecoming King for the 1973-74 school year.

And he became the first of Florencia's children to graduate.

In 1978, Richard was breaking rock underground at the San Manuel mine. He graduated to blasting and making tunnels.

"Back then, we worked underground at 2,600 feet. It was hard. I was scared all the time. Then after a while you don't get scared anymore. It's like working at Kmart."

But the hard work took its toll on him and others.

It was at San Manuel that Richard journeyed back to drugs.

"I got pulled into the cocaine. Then I got involved with this girl from Mammoth. I met her at a bar. She shot up in her veins. I tried it once, and the next thing you know, we were doing it all the time like that," he said.

He worked and functioned, but he was definitely hooked.

"I figured one of these days I was going to lay there and never wake up," he said.

He turned to Irene, who helped him get admitted to a drug rehabilitation center. He has stayed clean.

"I admire *Tía* for her strength. There is everything I put her through, what everybody — the world — put her through. Yet she can still stand up and say 'I'm here.'

"I love her. She is a solid rock. She probably will live forever."

Jaime: "*Tía* was always good to us. All my inner trouble was caused by memories of my dad."

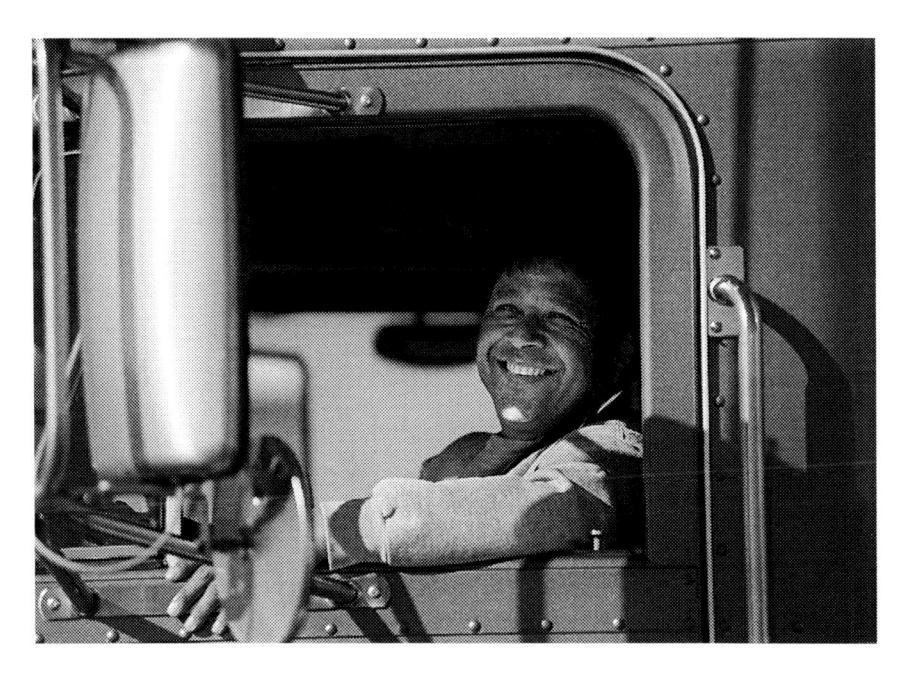

A weary trucker Raymond returns from a run to Amarillo, Texas. Photo by A.E. Araiza, Arizona Daily Star.

Chapter 34: Raymond and Carmen

Healthy fear of Mama kept us right on track

My brother Raymond and I toed the line, at least early in our lives.

We had the nuns and priests at St. John's instilling the fear of God in us. More important, we had the fear of Mama.

I hope I haven't given you the impression that Mama is some kind of softie who just oozes love all the time.

Mama was strict, and Mama was tough.

She kept on top of all our moves, and we have all felt her strap on occasion.

Raymond was an altar boy, whose idea of a wild time was sipping the altar wine.

"Bobby Gastellum and I used to fill up the cruets with water and wine. We used to take a swig every Sunday morning. Of course, this was without Father knowing, otherwise we would have been kicked out from the program," said Raymond.

During the week, we went to Mass every day before school.

Mama believed in spiritual nourishment. The Sisters of Charity, who operated the school, and the Holy Ghost Fathers, who ran the parish, made sure we got it.

Raymond listened. "I just let the Lord work on my mind. As I grew older, I think that's what really helped me out. The way Jesus handled certain things was really remarkable to me," said Raymond.

After Sunday Mass, when we were young, Raymond usually took off with Bobby and his cousin, Eddie León, to their grandparents. Francisco and Angelita León, who owned the rental where we lived, worked for grower Dan Clarke.

They took care of a farm just south of West Ajo Way, west of the river where cotton production halted and hay production began.

"Grandma and Grandpa León accepted me as one of their grandsons. We used to go play on the hay, sell hay, shoot pigeons, go fishing at their pond, drive the tractor, and do whatever was needed around the farm. I worked for Grandpa León and he would pay me," Raymond said.

In 1970, Raymond was in 10th grade at Pueblo High and stopped serving as an altar boy.

That same year he also stopped working at the Dairy Queen and for the next two summers he and Gabriel Barreda went to work in California. They lived with Gabe's sister in Huntington Beach, and Raymond worked to earn money to buy his school clothes.

His experience hoeing weeds in the cotton fields became useful in cleaning yards for wealthy families. Raymond also had fun.

The summer before he began his senior year, Raymond worked at a Mobil service station on West Congress Street, just east of Interstate 10. He watched the interstate truckers pulling on and off the freeway. He would become one of them eventually.

He hadn't thought about college because he wanted to join the Marines after graduation and fight in Vietnam. But the war was winding down when he graduated.

For myself, I didn't go away to work. I didn't go away, period.

Mama kept me at home.

"Mama, don't you trust me?" I'd ask. "I know how to be good."

She'd always reply, "I trust you. But it's others that I don't trust. You see, the devil never sleeps."

I couldn't figure out what she meant by that when I was a young girl.

Now, after years as crime reporter for the Star, I catch myself using that line when I talk to my nieces.

I always had to be home at the exact time she set, or I'd be punished. When it came to school activities, Mama was super liberal, but we had to stay up with our homework.

At St. John's, I was involved in volleyball and softball. In 1970, as a freshman at Pueblo High, it took me time to get used to going to a public school.

No more uniform, no more daily Mass, no more prayers in first period, and no more standing in line and filing into a classroom quietly.

I continued working at St. John's rectory on Saturdays until the summer before I started my junior year. Jane Otten and I went to work at der Weinerschnitzel on South Sixth Avenue. Except for the guy who tried to rob me at knifepoint one night, it was a pretty good job.

I was set to graduate from Pueblo High in 1974 with pretty good clerical skills. I wasn't thinking of college until Ralph Chavez, the founder of Pima Community College's journalism program, spoke to my journalism class about the need to integrate newsrooms. He also mentioned there might be scholarships available.

I told Mama. College wasn't even a thought to her, not something we could afford.

But a scholarship? "What do you have to lose?" said Mama.

I prayed to God and the *santos* to protect me and guide me. Mama prayed and lighted countless candles. I went to Pima where I worked for the Aztec Campus News. My love for journalism grew.

In the summers, I worked for the Summer Jobs for Youth program and did clerical work at the Veterans Affairs hospital. I graduated from Pima in 1976 and stopped going to school so I could work and save up money for a car and tuition at the University of Arizona.

I saved; Mama continued to clean motel rooms and pray. And she gambled. She won a $1,000 bingo jackpot at Sacred Heart Church. That helped me buy my first car and begin at the UA in 1978.

I received small scholarships from the Arizona Daily Star and the Tucson Press Club. I earned money while in college by working for Arizona Catholic Lifetime, the newspaper formerly published by the Roman Catholic Diocese of Tucson.

My last semester at the UA, I was hired as an intern at the Star. I graduated in December 1980 and was hired full-time at the Star in January 1981.

I was a real newspaper reporter, but I didn't feel like one immediately.

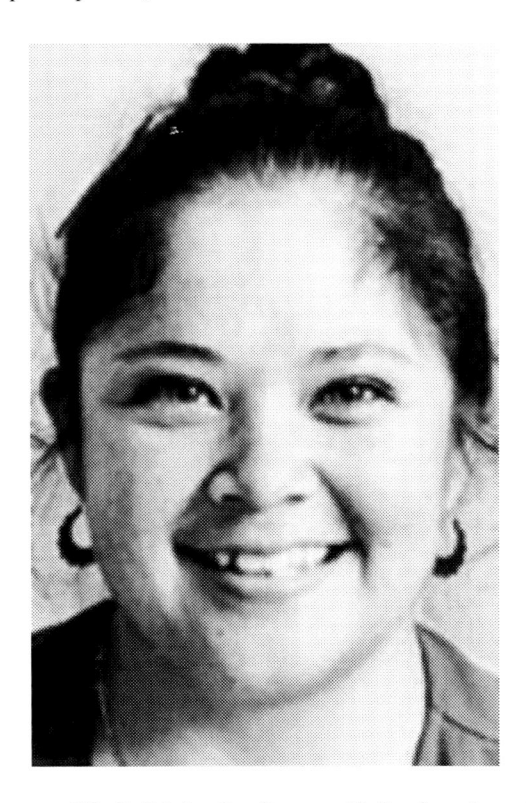

Author Carmen Duarte didn't think of college until the founder of Pima Community College's journalism program spoke to her class.

Nala's burial gown is a replica of the clothing worn in depictions of La Virgen de Guadalupe. Photo by A.E. Araiza, Arizona Daily Star.

Chapter 35: Life alone with Mama

A very sick and weak Nala is healed by faith, and Max

I didn't fit in right away at the Arizona Daily Star.

Part of it was my own insecurity, my inheritance from Mama.

Part was overhearing comments from some of my co-workers about how I and some other Hispanic and black journalists had been hired for our color or our ethnicity, not for our reporting and writing skills.

I thought: Maybe they're right.

Fortunately, there were people here who helped. City editor David McCumber pushed me to leave my post on Neighbors, a weekly section, and go to work writing daily news for the Metro section. Edie Auslander became a mentor, pushing me as well.

I started landing important assignments. I went to Mexico City several times. I followed the Sanctuary movement, an underground railroad composed of churches across the country that was sneaking Central American refugees into the United States and aiding them once they were here. Photographer Ron Medvescek and I even crossed the border illegally into the United States with them.

My stories appeared on the Front Page, and they mattered.

Pieces of my Sanctuary stories ended up in Esquire magazine and the New Yorker. Recruiters called from The Los Angeles Times and the Dallas Times Herald. I was one hot *chica*.

I stayed. Mama wouldn't leave Tucson. I wouldn't leave Mama.

But I became more secure and more comfortable here. This is my town. And this newspaper, well, now I feel like I own the place.

By 1982, Mama and I were alone in the rental on West President Street.

My four cousins had all moved on. My brother Raymond had gone to trucking school in Phoenix in 1976 and was driving 18-wheelers across the West, delivering soda to Texas, New Mexico and California and bales of cotton — cotton he once picked — to California for export.

All of Mama's *pollitos* had flown the nest — except me.

Mama never wanted me to go. There has always been a special bond between Mama and me. The bond solidified even more after Daddy's death in 1973.

It was the right thing to do. She had given of herself to everyone. It was my turn to give back to her.

I've had my fun working, dancing at nightclubs, and drinking way, way too much. I believe it was Mama's endless prayers to God and the *santos* that took care of me when I was younger and a *vata loca*.

I never crashed, and I made it home many nights who knows how. When I walked through the door, there was Mama devouring God and the *santos* with prayer, holding the rosary.

She was still cleaning motel rooms and needed her sleep. But, she'd stay awake praying until I made it home.

I can still hear her angry, yet relieved voice: *"Carmen, estás borracha. Ve y acuéstate."* ("Carmen, you're drunk. Go and lie down.")

Yes, I know it was her prayers that kept me safe.

In 1983, I lived and worked in Hermosillo, Sonora, for nearly three months, chronicling how our neighboring *compadres* survived the peso devaluation that was drowning the country.

I talked to Mama by telephone often and she never told me she was sick. She did not tell anyone.

When I returned, I found Mama pacing the floor like a woman gone mad, holding her rosary and scratching her left arm.

"I haven't slept for nights. Take me to the hospital," she said.

Mama hates hospitals. But she was crawling out of her skin, hallucinating — seeing snakes — as a result of medication she was taking for her gastrointestinal problems.

I called her doctor immediately and blasted him for not telling us about the side effects.

He called in a prescription to a pharmacy to counteract the hallucinations, and Mama was much better by morning. She stopped taking her medications cold turkey, and lost all faith in Western medicine.

Months passed. Mama had trouble passing food through her esophagus. She ate little and refused to see a doctor. She prayed. I worried. She grew weaker.

And she refused to stop working. I thought Mama was dying. I prayed to God for answers.

My *comadre*, Aida, told me about a man named Max who treated people with teas and herbal remedies.

Take Mama to an herbal healer? Back to the days of the *curanderos*?

I talked to Mama about Max and she perked up.

"It all has to do with faith. I believe in that, and I believe God will help me," she replied.

So, we were off to see Max.

Max was a dark-skinned, black-haired man who spoke with an almost eerie calmness. His brown eyes seemed to pierce my soul. I did not trust him, but Mama liked him immediately.

He ignored my questions. Be quiet and listen, he said.

Max studied Mama with his eyes. He said Mama was nervous and that I was the cause.

"Let her work if she wants to work. Back off," Max said.

How did he know that I was after Mama to stop working?

Max helped me to understand that work was life for Mama. She would die without work because she would feel useless.

I began taking Mama each week for her gallon of tea boiled from plants Max would find in the desert on the Tohono O'odham reservation.

Mama became stronger. She could eat and she was walking at a fast pace, head held high once again.

Mama was treated by Max for more than two years before he weaned her off the teas and told her she no longer needed him.

I ended up liking and trusting Max.

It took me a while to convince Mama to let me find her a medical doctor. When she started feeling sick again, she allowed me to take her.

She was so scared, but I found a good doctor who treated Mama and performed a yearly endoscopy, a little "Roto-Rooter" treatment for her esophagus.

In the early 1990s, medication was developed that has made it possible for Mama to eat all foods, and she no longer needs to go for her "Roto-Rooter" treatments.

In 1993, Mama finally quit cleaning toilets and making beds for strangers.

But she didn't quit on life. Her burial gown stayed packed away.

At age 77, she was needed at home to help raise a new family.

Nala's life has been one of almost unremitting hard labor, but also has been rich with the rewards of love and family. Though Nala began making preparations for her death decades ago, her work on Earth is not finished. In 1991, she found herself with three more children to raise, girls who once again filled her home with laughter.
Photo by A.E. Araiza, Arizona Daily Star.

Chapter 36: The meaning of it all

Tía Carmen follows in Mama's footsteps

I told you when I began this story that my Mama was making preparations to die, that she had begun doing so 34 years ago.

Her plans, *gracias a Dios*, kept getting interrupted.

The most recent interruption came in 1991 when, at age 74, Mama found herself with three more children to help raise.

Eventually, Mama and I helped my brother Raymond gain custody of his two daughters, Julisa and Clarissa.

Their half sister, Deana, also became part of our family.

Raymond and his girlfriend had split up. The girls needed a stable, loving environment, and they found it in our home, which I had bought in the mid-1980s.

Mama, Raymond and I began living life with renewed gusto. The girls brought a contagion of energy and laughter to our home.

There were also nights when I cried myself to sleep from pure exhaustion.

I was working a full day at home before heading to work to cover crime stories for the Star from 3 p.m. to midnight. Mama finally quit cleaning hotel rooms at age 77 to make sure she was home in time for me to go to work.

I came close to despair when all three girls broke out with chicken pox, and they took turns soaking in the tub with treatments to soothe their miserable, itching bodies.

But there was always an instant antidote to my self-pity. When I left for work, they would wrap their tiny arms around my legs, refuse to let go and say: "I love you, *Tía*."

So *Tía* Carmen learned to become a mama.

Boy, it's tough — being charged with molding children into responsible, loving adults who must learn to do the right thing, and also give back to their community.

It's a challenge for Raymond and me, but Mama is an excellent teacher in the science of unflappability.

She showed us that in 1996, shortly before her 80th birthday, five years after the girls moved in.

The girls' mother had accused Mama of child abuse.

Raymond and I were at work when Deana and Julisa began fighting and Mama tried to separate them.

They would not listen to her, so Mama picked up a plastic toy bat and whacked Deana on the leg. It left a bruise.

During the fight, Julisa, then 8, had scratched Deana, 9, below one eye.

After the girls' mother saw Deana's bruise and scratch, she went to school the next day, took all three girls home and called the police.

I came home that evening and listened in horror as Mama told a police officer on the phone. "Yes, I hit her. Yes, I hit her with a baseball bat."

"Mama," I said. "Explain to the officer that it is a plastic toy bat."

Mama hung up and said an officer was on her way to pick up the bat.

I was a nervous wreck — picturing Mama being taken away in handcuffs, photographed and locked up in jail.

"Carmen," Mama asked, "don't you have any faith? God will protect me. I did what I had to do. The girls know the truth."

Mama was right again. Everyone told the truth. Detectives investigated and found no cause for charges.

Julisa and Clarissa came back home, but the girls' mother kept Deana.

We had no legal recourse since Deana has no blood ties. So after five years in our home, suddenly our baby, Deana, was gone. A part of me died that day.

But, over time, we began to see her more. She is still a part of the family. She knows she always will be our baby.

Mama always tells me, "You don't have control over everything. Leave it to God. It is up to him, not you."

Mama's advice is consistent and wise. I've begun reciting it back to her.

Mama's heart was broken a couple of years back when Raymond switched religions.

He made Julisa and Clarissa stop going to religious-education classes at St. John the Evangelist Catholic Church. He made them leave the altar server program and took the girls with him to an eastside Baptist church.

Raymond had developed some problems with praying to saints and the Blessed Mother.

The girls liked the Baptist services at first, but after several months they preferred to go to Mass. Raymond allowed that.

Mama prayed to God and the *santos* for Raymond to come back to the Catholic faith, and he went to Mass with us occasionally.

I tell Mama there is one God, and there are many faiths. If the girls follow God's commands about loving him and loving one another, they will be fine.

Mama listens but keeps praying for their return to her faith.

One Saturday morning, I smiled and felt warm inside as my nieces, Deana, Julisa and Clarissa, and their friend, Angelica, kissed me goodbye and walked out the front door.

They climbed into the van with my brother, Raymond, and headed to Tucson High Magnet School.

The girls — all Wakefield Middle School students — were meeting other students from around the city who were volunteering to paint over graffiti.

Our *pollitos* were giving back to the community.

I wiped happy and proud tears, and walked back into the house where Mama was washing the breakfast dishes.

That pretty much brings us up to date. It's time for Mama and me to say *adiós*. I'll go first.

Carmen Duarte helped provide a stable, loving environment for her nieces Julisa, left, Clarissa and Deana; together, they brought new life to the household.

• • •

Mama's strength flows in my veins. Her faith is mine. Her teachings have made me who I am.

So who am I?

I am a woman, born in Tucson, who, as a child, picked cotton and pecans not far from my south side neighborhood.

I am a woman who, as a girl, helped Mama clean hotel rooms.

I am a woman who lives in a barrio that is feared by some.

I am a woman who loves children and wants to share with them stories I've covered over the years working at the Star.

I am a woman who expects great things from my nieces, my *pollitos*. I challenge them to work hard in school and want them to understand that each of them is important. They are our future. They need to stand up and be counted.

I am a woman who still believes in the goodness of human beings and who knows that God expects us to love one another and better our world.

At times, though, I am tired. I am tired of trying to educate people who only see my barrio as ugly and depressed, full of people who live on government handouts and youth who are nothing but gangbangers.

I try not to despair. I lean on God and listen to Mama's voice:

"Mi hijita, no te angusties. Ponte fuerte y lista. Mañana es otro día y Dios está contigo." (My little daughter, don't anguish. Get strong and be ready. Tomorrow is another day, and God is with you.)

I also can hear Mama's other voice. The one that makes me laugh.

"Porqué lloras? Como eres chillona. Tú sabes que el mundo está lleno de babosos. Dios sabe eso." (Why are you crying? You are such a crybaby. You know that the world is full of idiots. God knows that.)

You are right, Mama.

But there is so much more work that needs to be done. We need more youth to graduate and go to college. We need no more youth filling our prisons. We need no more teen-agers becoming parents.

So I place my faith in God and the future.

My nieces and cousins are armed with *la familia*'s faith and its strength.

We are many. Relatives estimate that our extended family easily numbers more than 1,000.

Some are already making a difference as counselors, educators, engineers, executives, police, a defense lawyer and a federal judge.

And one is a journalist who cries through half her stories.

The time has come for this *chillona* to sadly say goodbye to "Mama's Santos," a project that taught me so much about myself, *mi gente y mi linda Madre*.

I know my Mama is proud of me, though any time she speaks of my profession, she said I spend my days gathering *mitotes*, gossip.

But hey, I'm the queen of *mitotes*.

And I'm grateful for this chance to tell my Mama's story. *Gracias, Mama. Gracias a todos.*

Trucker Raymond spends most of his time on the road, which means his girls are in the care of his sister, series author Carmen Duarte, and his Mama Leonarda. Raymond's switching of religions did not sit well with Mama.

• • •

    Now it's Mama's turn and, as usual, she is reluctant.
    She was making supper when I asked her to tell us all the meaning of her life.
    She gave me one of those looks. You know, the look that said "What idiotic question are you asking now?"
    She stopped cutting a tomato into wedges and her forehead wrinkled. She became annoyed.
    "Mi trabajo es hacer la caridad, yo no ando filosoficando. Mi vida es mi vida y eso es todo." (My work is to be kind, and I am not philosophizing. My life is my life, and that is all.)
    I should have known. Mama does not talk in the abstract. She acts. She believes there are too many idiots who talk and do nothing.
    "God shows me the way. He doesn't come down and talk to me like you talk to me. I pray to him and things happen. He forgives me, but he has no time to talk to a sinner like me. He has heard me all the times my *pollitos* were in trouble, and he helped me."
    "I have lived a long life because God has me here. People need to understand that they have to give of themselves to God and he will take care of them."
    Mama begins cutting the tomato again and continues, I guess you would say, theologizing:

"The devil is among us, and he is the one who at all times is seeing where he can stick his tail."

"Things happen for a reason. People who get angry at God are crazy. God knows what he does. And, like the saying goes: 'God punishes without (using) a stick or a whip.'"

For Mama, the present is the best time of her life.

"I do what I want. When I lived with my mother, I did what she said. God took care of me. After I left my mother, I lived with my older sisters and took care of my younger brothers and sisters. When I got married, I raised my children and my sister's children. I taught all of you the best I could. God guided me all of my life.

"My granddaughters are now my life. I love them as though they were my children. When they are not here at home, it is as though a part of me is not here.

"I want my granddaughters to do their best and aim high. I want them to go to school and do the best they can with their lives. They have a good chance to achieve whatever they want.

"I want them to believe in God and the *santos*, and know they are there for them," Mama said.

"I am in my glory on Earth," said Mama, "and when I die, I hope to be in my glory in heaven."

Mama Leonarda's words of wisdom: "People need to understand that they have to give of themselves to God and he will take care of them."

Epilogue

Mama's years of preparation to die ended March 5, 2007.
Leonarda "Nala" Bejarano Duarte's obituary from the March 6, 2007, Arizona Daily Star and the funeral notice from March 8, 2007, follow.

'An Arizona Life' ends for 'Nala' Duarte, 90

By Tom Beal
Arizona Daily Star

Leonarda Bejarano Duarte, whose life of hard work, faith and endurance was lovingly told by her daughter, Carmen Duarte, in the Arizona Daily Star series "Mama's Santos: An Arizona Life," died Monday at age 90.

Duarte faced her death with the same calm acceptance and strong faith with which she lived her life.

When the doctor told her recently that she had stomach cancer, she waited for her daughter to translate his words into Spanish and replied simply: "Well, we all have to die of something."

On Sunday, as her life force waned, she insisted on going to church, and Carmen Duarte reluctantly loaded her mama into the car and wheeled her to the front of St. John the Evangelist Catholic Church on West Ajo Way, where she breathed rapidly through the service.

Afterward, the Rev. Robert Gonzalez came and said: "Leonarda, I'm going to anoint you with oil," offering her the sacrament of the sick, the final sacrament of the Catholic faith she had embraced all her life.

Father Gonzalez said he had watched Duarte throughout the service. To him, she was obviously near death, but he said her eyes were shining with the certainty of those "for whom the Lord is our light and salvation."

And he was thinking of Duarte when he told the congregation that "these individuals don't fear anything, not sickness nor impending death. I just saw her as a woman of great faith and great principle who exemplified the beauty of that generation - the strong Hispanic woman."

Sunday night, Carmen slept with her mom, turning her when she had difficulty breathing.

In early morning, Carmen called for her nieces, Leonarda's granddaughters Julisa and Clarissa, to come and say goodbye.

Leonarda "Nala" Bejarano was born Sept. 18, 1916, in Virden, N.M., two months after her father, Ambrosio Bejarano, had been struck and killed by lightning while working in the fields along the Gila River. His wife, Dolores, was left with five children to raise.

Leonarda spent little time in school, completing fourth grade at the Mexican School in Duncan, going to the fields to pick cotton as early as age 9, and becoming the woman of the dirt-floored home at age 11.

She survived a fire that consumed the family home and a fever that killed many in the Gila River Valley in 1929. By age 16, she was working the fields full time. She later worked as a housekeeper in Duncan and cleaned miners' dormitories in Morenci.

After World War II, she moved with her brother Florentino to Tucson and continued working in the fields in Midvale Park and Marana. She had two children, Carmen and Raymond, after marrying fellow picker Federico Duarte.

She ended up raising the children mostly on her own, and after her sister Florencia died of tuberculosis, she added Florencia's four children to the family. They lived in a one-bedroom house on Tucson's South Side, and Duarte supported the family by cotton-picking, housekeeping and cleaning motel rooms.

She would later tell her daughter the journalist that she saw nothing remarkable about her life, and she resisted retelling it.

But Carmen's 36-part series resonated profoundly in Tucson, where many readers found it a retelling of their own families' first-generation tales of hard work, faith and perseverance.

The series was honored nationally, and Duarte was named Journalist of the Year by the National Association of Hispanic Journalists. It became part of the Mexican-American Studies curriculum in the Tucson Unified School District.

The first words of the series, published in 2000, were: "Mama is preparing to die."

She had chosen her rosary, and she had commissioned a burial gown to replicate the red-and-green robe worn in depictions of *La Virgen de Guadalupe*. Surrounded by her *santos* (images of Catholic saints), Leonarda Duarte was always ready to meet God.

The last words of the series were a quote from her: "I am in my glory on Earth, and when I die, I hope to be in my glory in heaven."

She is survived by her brother, Juan Téllez; children, Carmen and Raymond; grandchildren, Julisa Duarte, Clarissa Duarte and Deana Sanchez; and great-grandson, Brandon Sanchez. Other survivors include her sister's children whom she raised: Raúl (Mary) Herrera, Irene (George) Romero, Jaime (Shelly) Herrera and Richard Herrera.

Duarte asked before she died that any remembrances be made to the poor, in the form of food or cash donations to the Community Food Bank or Casa San Juan, the charitable arm of her parish church.

Services will be Friday at St. John the Evangelist Catholic Church, 602 W. Ajo Way, with a viewing beginning at 9:30 a.m., rosary at 10:30 a.m. and Mass at 11 a.m., concelebrated by Father Gonzalez and the Rev. Raúl Trevizo.

Funeral Notices

Leonarda "Nala" Bejarano Duarte
September 18, 1916 — March 5, 2007

    Nala was born in Virden, New Mexico, and grew up in the Gila River Valley. She moved to Tucson in the early 1950s and married Federico Duarte in Nogales, AZ. She raised son, Raymond and daughter, Carmen and her sister's children Raúl (Mary) Herrera, Irene (George) Romero, Jaime (Shelly) Herrera and Richard Herrera. But many others, including granddaughters, Deana (son, Brandon), Julisa, Clarissa; her nieces, nephews, grand-nieces and grand-nephews all loved Nala as a mother and grandmother. She touched many people, and she taught them all that God is first, family second and community third. Her motto in life was that we have to help each other and do what is right. She believed that no child asked to be born, so parents had to be responsible and raise their children to be good, productive people who would give to their community. Nala showed her love through cooking. Anyone who came to her house, she would feed. She loved to bake and will be remembered for her yeast bread, lemon meringue pies, her chocolate pudding pies topped with bananas and her doughnuts. She was well known for her spicy red chile con carne *tamales*, homemade *tortillas* with butter, her caldos, and the Lenten foods, such as cheese enchiladas, *nopalitos* with red chile, *calabacitas con queso* and her *capirotada* (bread pudding). Because of this, the family is asking that donations be made in her memory to the Community Food Bank or Casa de San Juan, which helps immigrants, at St. John the Evangelist Catholic Church. Services will be Friday at St. John the Evangelist Catholic Church, 602 W. Ajo Way, with a viewing beginning at 9:30 a.m., Rosary at 10:30 a.m. and Mass at 11a.m., concelebrated by Revs. Robert Gonzalez and Raúl Trevizo. Burial will follow at Holy Hope Cemetery, 3555 N. Oracle Road. Funeral services entrusted to Martinez Funeral Chapels, 2580 S. Sixth Ave., South Tucson, AZ.

Awards for 'Mama's Santos'

The "Mama's Santos" series received the following awards and citations:

Chicanos por La Causa's Individual Award (2000)

Inland Press Association's First Place Award for Community Leadership (2000)

Hispanic Professional Action Committee's Woman of the Year (2000)

Arizona Associated Press Managing Editors Association's Second Place Award in Enterprise Reporting (2000)

Arizona Newspapers Foundation's Honorable Mention for Community Service/Journalistic Achievement (2000)

Columbia University Graduate School of Journalism's 2001 Let's Do It Better honoree (race and ethnic reporting)

National Association of Hispanic Journalists (2001) public service award and Guillermo Martinez-Marquez Award for Overall Excellence.

Inter American Press Association, first place (tie) for feature writing (2001).

2001 University of Missouri Lifestyle Journalism Award, multicultural category.

2001 FBI Community Service Award for "outstanding and dedicated service to our community."

Contributors

Series editor: Tom Beal
Cover photo/photographer: A.E. Araiza
Additional photography: Aaron J. Latham
E-book/Espresso book machine editor: Ann Brown
E-book/Espresso book cover design: Tammie Graves
Series copy editors: Ron Solomon, Mark Stewart
E-book/Espresso book machine copy editor: John Bolton
Visual Team Leader/Photography, Arizona Daily Star: Rick Wiley
Editor, Arizona Daily Star: Bobbie Jo Buel

"Mama's Santos" primary photographer A.E. Araiza, left, series editor Tom Beal and author Carmen Duarte.